A Partnership for

THE SUPERVISION OF STUDENT TEACHERS

by

Duaine C. Lang
Coordinator, Office of Field Experiences
Indiana University

and

Alan F. Quick
Director of Student and Intern Teaching
Central Michigan University

and

James A. Johnson
Director of Clinical Experiences
Northern Illinois University

The Great Lakes Publishing Company
Mt. Pleasant, Michigan

Table of Contents

CONTENTS

CONTENTS

CONTENTS

Preface

This book contains what we believe about student teaching and teacher preparation. In addition to accepting the commonly acknowledged value of student teaching and other clinical experiences in teacher education, we believe that:

1.) Teacher Education students (observers, participants, student teachers, interns, and practicum students) can have a direct and *positive* effect on pupil learning.

2.) The only realistic setting for the translation of theory into practice is the laboratory provided by the public and private elementary and secondary schools and the communities they serve.

3.) The previous goal can be only achieved through a partnership effort on the part of teacher preparing institutions and the cooperating schools—a partnership that functions in reality, totality, and equality to a degree far in excess of what has been achieved to date in most locales.

4.) Supervision is the sum total of the activities of all persons involved in the learning activities of teacher education students, including the students themselves.

5.) A teacher teaches primarily as he was taught. This places the responsibility for change first upon us as learners and teachers and secondly upon the students we prepare.

6.) The focus of all teacher preparation, and in particular field experiences, should be on "learning to teach" as opposed to "practice" or "modeling." This focus is best accomplished when the experiences provide for:

   a.) sequential development spread through the entire preparation program.

   b.) development in terms of specific course and experiences relationships.

   c.) individualization, beyond the variables of time and place, so as to capitalize upon the individual needs and talents of prospective teachers and the schools and pupils they will serve.

   d.) a completeness of immersion which features a constant stress on the provision of realism.

   e.) alternative patterns of preparation, most of which concentrate upon developed or emergent instructional thrusts in the schools.

f.) concern with the "why" as opposed to the "how" of instructional efficiency and effectiveness.

g.) an introduction to and training in self-improvement techniques so as to avoid the finality of continued growth that is now commonly associated with preparation programs.

We sincerely hope that this book will be of value to those teacher educators throughout the United States who supervise teacher education students in a wide variety of clinical experiences. We are also endebted to the considerable number of these teacher educators who have helped mold our beliefs about student teaching which are presented in this volume.

J.J.
A.Q.
D.L.

CHAPTER ONE

The Historical Development of Clinical Experiences in Teacher Education

You ask me what I aimed to accomplish and would aim to accomplish now, with my past experience before me in a normal school. I would answer briefly that it is my aim, and it would be my aim again, to make better teachers, and especially better teachers for our common schools . . . teachers who would know more of the nature of children, of youthful development, more of the subjects to be taught, and more of the methods of teaching them . . . In short, I was desirous of putting our schools in the hands of those who would make them places in which children could learn, not only to read and write and spell and cipher, but where they would have all their faculties trained in such harmony as would result in the highest formation of character.

> Cyrus Pierce, First Principal of the Lexington, Massachusetts Normal School writing to Henry Barnard, in 1851. Quoted in: *Public Education in the United States*. Ellwood P. Cubberley, (Boston, Houghton, Mifflin, Co., 1947), p. 381

Times Have Changed

Although the first normal school originated in 1823 as a private endeavor, it wasn't until 1839 that the Lexington, Massachusetts Normal School opened. In 1851, Cyrus Pierce established a school to prepare teachers and for his time he was highly successful. Yet the evolution of such a school and the accompanying training necessary to prepare teachers was an extremely slow process.

It doesn't seem possible to many of us that teacher education programs and teacher education institutions in the United States date back one hundred and fifty years. For today we are blessed with excellent teacher education facilities. Future teachers are prepared in a four year college or university environment which emphasizes general education, major and minor development, and professional education courses and experi-

1

ences. The professional education sequence is a blend of theory and practice with every effort made to bridge the distance between the two. Clinical experiences, or those experiences which provide the future teacher with opportunities to work with students in a public or private school environment, are planned and supervised cooperatively by college and K-12 district personnel. Cooperating classroom teachers frequently receive preparation to better enable them to supervise students in a clinical experience. More than ever before they have more voice in the sequence of courses leading to initial certification of teachers. College supervisors of clinical experiences are most often full-time faculty members of a department or college of education and are more committed, better prepared, and have a better support base from the college than ever before in history. Times are not perfect in contemporary education—but we have traveled a long continuous path of improvement in teacher education. One does not have to probe too far back in history to realize that not so long ago it was far different. Schools reflect the times, and the times have changed greatly.

The authors feel that in order to appreciate and understand the present, an understanding of the past is necessary. The educational history of Americans, much like the American past itself, is a stirring record of achievements in the face of difficulty. It records the promise of American life. The intent of this chapter is to sketch briefly the development of the clinical experience phase of teacher education from its beginning of the small teacher education class organized and taught by Father Charles Demia in Lyon, France in 1672[1] to today's vast partnership arrangement involving thousands of K-12 district personnel who cooperate with colleges to prepare educators for today's classrooms.

EARLY ATTEMPTS TO PREPARE TEACHERS

Incidental Training

Prior to the 1700's, a knowledge of how and what to teach was usually transmitted in an incidental fashion. For instance, in the very earliest of times, the first teachers were those especially proficient in hunting, fishing, or the making of weapons. Knowingly or unknowingly, these tribal members who had gained a high degree of proficiency in these areas became the teachers of youth in the immediate area. Gradually as these early tribes became more structured, the most powerful figure in the tribe was often the teacher. Although these teachers were called

[1] Cubberley, Ellwood P., *Public Education in the United States,* (Boston, Houghton Mifflin Co., 1947) p. 371.

medicine men, wizards, or witch doctors, they were given the difficult yet very important responsibility of appeasing the various spirits who brought sorrow or unhappiness to the tribe. To help do this they developed dances, chants and other methods to insure rain, sunlight, protection, and good health. In addition to developing time-proven methods to propitiate the spirits, they were obligated to pass them on to prospective medicine men within the tribe. Potentially talented youngsters were then selected to learn the secret rites. The medicine men taught them the necessary secrets. The chosen youngsters would then practice and preserve the secrets of the tribe and, in turn, pass them on to another generation. This was a very early and rudimentary attempt to transfer a body of knowledge from one person to another.

The Apprenticeship Method

As society, particularly vocations, became more complex, the method of learning from others was translated into the apprenticeship method. Apprenticeship was based upon the idea of observing and learning by doing while serving under a proven master. This method of learning was especially popular during the Middle Ages (476 A.D.–1300 A.D.). Gradually laws were passed which bound the apprentice to a master for a set length of time and obligated the apprentice to the master and his family. Later in the 1600's when compulsory education laws were passed, masters were often required not only to teach apprentices a trade but also the fundamentals of reading and writing. Although such laws were passed, the requirement that an apprentice be taught to read and write was easier said than done. The growing need for efficient knowledge transfer and translation brought about the first organized formal attempt to teach individuals how to teach effectively.

The Church

Prior to 1700, the Church, the family, or the master of the apprentice, were the prime educational agencies. Church leaders, realizing the need for formalized education classes to help priests interpret religious matters to others, developed small classes for this purpose. Father Charles Demia in France was one of the first to do this. Because Demia was dissatisfied with the inadequate teaching methods of a group of volunteer teachers, he organized a class whereby the volunteers could learn his ideas and teaching methods which he felt were effective. Other Church classes designed to improve teaching effectiveness were developed during the 17th and 18th centuries. In 1685 in Rhiems, France, a teaching institution was founded to prepare teachers for the schools of a religious order.

This school, founded by Jean Baptiste de la Salle, was primarily designed for the preparation of elementary teachers. To more effectively prepare elementary teachers, de la Salle opened another school in Paris for the sole purpose of providing student teaching. (These previously mentioned schools are considered by many historians to be the first teacher training schools.)

The Prussian Influence

Several German states, and especially Prussia, were world leaders in educational ideas and organizational patterns following the Protestant Reformation of 1517. A Lutheran clergyman, August Herman Francke, in 1696 established what many educational historians consider to be the first teacher education institution in Germany. Francke's school was located at Halle and was called a Seminarium Praeceptorum.[2] In the beginning Francke prepared only elementary teachers but later expanded his schools to include the preparation of secondary teachers. At the time of his death the seminarium praeceptorum included 2,341 pupils and 175 teachers. Francke's contributions added emphasis to the importance of preparing a teacher while he worked in a school environment under the supervision of an experienced teacher. Another Prussian, Julius Heckel, urged the Prussian government to establish teacher education institutions throughout the state. By the middle of the 19th century, when Americans were first giving serious thought to the establishment of institutions specifically designed for teachers, Prussian institutions served as models.

Historical Figures Influence Teacher Education

Throughout the 1700's, educational and social theorists exerted a great influence upon teacher education. In 1762 Jean Jacques Rousseau, a French writer and political philosopher, wrote a novel entitled *Emile* which was concerned with the education of a young man. In the novel Rousseau described the type of education that he desired and emphasized that education should encourage self-expression, instead of the harsh discipline and regimentation customary in the schools of the day. Johann Heinrich Pestalozzi, a German Swiss, was greatly influenced by *Emile*, and saw the need for carefully prepared teachers in "the science and art" of teaching. Pestalozzi believed that education should be based upon the natural development of the child and should stress moral and physical as well as intellectual development. To test his theories,

---

[2] Johnson, James A., *A Brief History of Student Teaching*. (De Kalb: Creative Educational materials, 1968), p. 14.

It is evident that this 16th century classroom depicts the "Science and Art of Teaching."

Pestalozzi converted a farm into a school for poor children. Unfortunately the school failed because of financial difficulties, but Pestalozzi's several books, including *Leonard and Gertrude,* resulted in the organization in 1799 of an institute for training teachers. Statesmen and educators from many parts of the world, including the United States, came to study his methods and ideas.

Two Germans, Johann Friedrich Herbart and Friedrich Froebel, were impressed with Pestalozzi's work. After visiting Pestalozzi's institute, Herbart experimented with some of antecedent (Pestalozzi's) ideas which helped him greatly in formulating his own—later called the Herbartian method. Herbart felt that students must be interested in education and that teachers had the responsibility for motivating them. Herbart, to provide a forum for his ideas concerning methodology, introduced a seminar in pedagogy and a practice school where teachers could work under his supervision. Friedrich Froebel, the founder of the kindergarten, felt that a teacher should cooperate with nature and guide the functions of the child as the impulses develop. He reasoned that children learn by doing things, and their play should be organized to teach as well as to amuse. To promote his educational ideas, Froebel established a number of teacher training classes. The students in these classes usually took part in a form of practice teaching by working with kindergarten children.

Two other individuals who contributed ideas to the development of teacher education institutions in the United States were Andrew Bell and Joseph Lancaster. These Britishers, in the 1790's, developed a system whereby a great number of students could be taught by a single teacher.[3] This extremely economical method of teaching from 100 to 1000 students in a large hall appealed to many because of its cheapness. By utilizing monitors, or those older and better students, to act as teacher aides, many youngsters who might never have had the opportunity for any education were able to attend school. When this method was brought to America it caused quite a sensation; in the beginning it was lauded as a fine method of education. Gradually its charm diminished and its glaring deficiencies became evident. It was a cheap method of mass educating and was soon discarded. Many of the monitors, however, were motivated to become regular teachers and their experience as monitors served as a form of practice teaching.

TEACHER EDUCATION IN COLONIAL AMERICA

Little Teacher Education in Colonial America

Although the previously mentioned individuals were concerned with teaching methodology and seminars were taught by them to translate their concern to others, the great majority of teachers in the eighteenth and nineteenth centuries did not receive any formal teacher training.

Most educational historians feel that the reason for this was that most of the settlers in the 17th and 18th centuries came from England, and teacher education had not made much headway in that country.

After the War of 1812 and the accompanying stabilizing of government and economy, a few United States educators began advocating teacher education institutions. During the 1820's and 1830's a vigorous campaign developed in the United States toward the establishment of teacher education institutions. Inasmuch as European institutions were used as examples and European Normal Schools had model schools and practice teaching as an integral part, it was only natural that Americans adopted this plan.

The campaign to obtain teacher education schools culminated in 1823 in Concord, Vermont, when the Reverend Samuel Hall established a private institution to prepare teachers.[4] Hall offered a three year course

[3] Ibid., p. 19.

[4] Cubberley, *Public Education in the United States*, p. 325.

which included observation and student teaching during the winter in rural schools. In addition to starting the first teacher training institution in the United States, Hall, in all probability, wrote the first professional education book written and published in the United States. The book, entitled *Lectures on School Keeping,* was published in 1829.

THE DEVELOPMENT OF TEACHER TRAINING INSTITUTIONS IN THE UNITED STATES

Evolution of Early State Teacher Training Institutions

The first state teacher training school in the United States opened on July 3, 1839 in Lexington, Massachusetts, after several years of advocacy by James G. Carter and Horace Mann. Carter, a member of the Massachusetts State Legislature, along with Mann, the Secretary of the Massachusetts State Board of Education, realized the need for a state institution to prepare teachers and persuaded others to concur. A wealthy Boston merchant named Edmund Dwight offered to provide a gift of $10,000 for the establishment of a teacher training school if the state would match the gift.[5] The result was the passage of a state law and the beginning of state teacher education institutions in the United States. The name "normal school" was selected for the Lexington institution from the French *ecoles normales primaires* which was the term applied to similar institutions in France.

From the beginning it appears that Cyrus Pierce, the first Principal of the Lexington Normal School, was convinced of the value and necessity for providing demonstration, observation, participation, and practice teaching experiences for the future teachers attending the Lexington Normal School. The Lexington Normal School, because of excellent leadership on the part of Pierce, exerted great influence upon other normal schools later established in the United States.

For various reasons, however, the early normal schools and their adjoining practice schools were not popular when they were first established, and many of the legislators of Massachusetts were negative in their feelings towards the schools. Some who were against the movement felt that it was an attempt to "Prussianize the schools," while others argued that there was no need for practice schools because the academies (the forerunner of the American high schools) were doing an excellent job of teacher training. While it is true that the academies often offered a course designed to help teachers teach, this was not their prime objective nor did they include any practice teaching.

[5] Ibid., p. 379.

In addition there were those who feared and misunderstood the functions of the normal schools. Opponents of the public school movement which developed concurrently with the normal school movement were especially fearful that these schools would promote public schools. Despite these problems, however, the normal schools survived and expanded. New York established a school in 1844; Connecticut and Michigan followed in 1849.

The work of David Page, Principal of the Albany Normal School in New York, was particularly influential in encouraging the practice teaching aspect of the normal school. Page emphasized actual practice teaching under real classroom conditions. Each pupil was given an opportunity to practice methods of instruction and to have other teaching responsibilities at the Albany Normal School.

Besides the contributions of Page, the work of Edward A. Sheldon at the Oswego State Normal School which opened in 1861 in Oswego, New York, is particularly noteworthy. Sheldon, utilizing Pestalozzian methods, gained national acclaim for the preparation of teachers. This was especially true when a number of educators visited the school and departed convinced that skill in the method of teaching was as important as subject matter competence. This feeling caused other educators to concentrate on the art of teaching and added impetus to practice teaching. Graduates of the Oswego Normal School were in great demand and soon filled many key positions in teacher education throughout the United States.

State legislation grew slowly in encouraging the development of teacher training institutions. By the end of the 1850's only twelve normal schools supported by state funds had been established in Massachusetts, New York, Connecticut, Rhode Island, New Jersey, Pennsylvania, Michigan, Illinois, and Minnesota. Besides these scattered endeavors, a number of municipalities undertook to run their own normal school. Boston and New York established schools for girls to prepare them for positions in the common schools. By 1875, there were sixty-seven normal schools, with forty-seven training schools used primarily for practice teaching. One should not get the feeling though that normal schools were making much headway either in growth or academic reputation. The demands put upon its learners were not high. The normal school was actually little more than a higher elementary school, and the work of the school spanned a year and in unusual situations, two years. Much of the time spent in school was devoted to elementary learning and the study of how to teach became subordinate. Pedagogy in America moved into the 20th century in a sorry state of affairs.

By 1900, forty-four states had established normal schools and the idea that teachers needed some special training was gaining momentum.

At the turn of the century all the Normal Schools together graduated no more than one-fourth of the new teachers. Normal schools received some help in the preparation of teachers as universities began establishing departments of education. During the last third of the nineteenth century one of the very earliest to do so was the University of Iowa which established an education department when it opened in 1855. In 1878 Iowa expanded the department into a College of Normal Instruction and in 1907 it became a School of Education. Gradually the idea was widely accepted. By 1900 many colleges and universities throughout the country had instituted a Normal Department.

Although these institutions were used primarily to prepare elementary teachers, formal preparation in normal schools or departments of a university was not necessary to obtain a teaching position. Thus, at the beginning of the 20th century, the great mass of elementary school teachers had studied in neither Normal Schools or Normal Departments in universities. In fact, they had no formal preparation to become teachers. Certification standards for teachers were generally extremely low.

THE LABORATORY SCHOOL MOVEMENT

The College Laboratory Schools Rise and Fall

The development of student teaching during the first forty years of the 20th century generally centers around the importance of the model school or laboratory school. In 1926 the American Association of Teachers Colleges established standards for accreditation of teacher education institutions. Two standards were adopted which promoted the development of the laboratory school and student teaching; each teacher's college should maintain a training school or equivalent facilities, and a minimum of ninety hours of student teaching be required for each student.[6]

Initially, it was felt that laboratory schools should duplicate the typical elementary school and provide the Normal School with immediate and total access to students and facilities. With this in mind each laboratory school stressed demonstration, observation, and student teaching. As the twentieth century progressed, however, some college laboratory schools expanded and became centers for educational experimentation, but unfortunately, as history will record, most remained centers for demonstration and student teaching.

Most early laboratory schools employed the services of highly qualified

[6]Quick, Donald M. *A Historical Study of The Campus Laboratory Schools in Four Teacher Education Institutions in Michigan.* (Unpublished Doctoral thesis, School of Education, The University of Michigan, 1970), pp. 26.

and expert teachers who served not only as supervising teachers to neophytes, but also as models for the other teachers in the area. Students who practice-taught in the laboratory schools received highly structured supervision and often left the laboratory school blessed with the philosophy and teaching techniques of the laboratory school supervising teacher.

Gradually, the laboratory school and its relationship to the teacher education institution was challenged. It became increasingly more difficult for college administrators to justify the cost factor of the laboratory school because the public school environment frequently was equal in facilities and quality of teaching. When Normal Schools made the transition to Colleges of Education and grew considerably after World War II, the Laboratory School was usually not large enough to accommodate the numbers of students who needed a student teaching assignment. Because of growth and the fact that most laboratory schools failed to be research-oriented, and because the public school environment provided a much more flexible and realistic environment for student teachers, colleges—during the 1950's and 1960's—turned to public schools to provide observational, participational, and student teaching experiences for prospective teachers. Laboratory schools did serve a very useful purpose during their era and greatly contributed to the improvement of teaching.

EARLY ATTEMPTS AT PUBLIC SCHOOL—COLLEGE COOPERATIVE TEACHER EDUCATION PROGRAMS

The Colleges Fail to Establish a Sound Foundation for Cooperative Programs.

Although the colleges turned to the public and private school environment to use as student teaching locations, a sound basis for this type of situation did not exist. Classroom teachers often, without their prior consent, had a student teacher from a nearby college placed in their classroom by an obliging public school administrator. Even when classroom teachers knew that they were having student teachers the atmosphere of acceptance on the part of the classroom teachers was not always positive. The classroom teacher often felt unprepared to work effectively with a student teacher. In addition to inadequate communication, preparation and interpretation of the program, other problems existed.

Some public school administrators accepted student teachers for recruiting reasons or because one or more of the classroom teachers had an extra large group or an unusually unruly class. These reasons for accepting student teachers usually did not contribute to meaningful learning experiences for student teachers.

The college-public-private school relationship often got off to a bad start for other reasons. Students were usually placed in a public school environment without any thought of on-site college supervision, and, to compound the problem, very few materials were developed to aid the classroom teacher to successfully supervise. When colleges did provide a liaison person to work with the public schools and private schools, professors of education who taught the theory, methodology, history and philosophy of education on campus were contemptuous of their colleagues working with student teachers. The lack of college supervision, support of the cooperating teacher, and the low esteem of the college supervisor, contributed to strained relationships between K-12 school personnel and those working in the college. In spite of these problems, however, student teaching in K-12 schools grew rapidly during the 1950's and 1960's and was regarded by most students as the single most important experience in their teacher education program. Prospective teachers often regarded their supervising teacher as the individual who helped them the most in becoming a successful teacher.

THE DILEMMA OF THE 1960's

Teacher Concern and Power

As the teaching profession gained power through the development of strong unions and the labor negotiation process during the 1960's, participating public school teachers demanded a teacher education program which included their involvement and a greater adherence to professional responsibility in student teaching on the part of the college. As the nucleus of the demands appeared to be directed at greater financial remuneration for the classroom teacher's role in working with prospective teachers, the colleges with meager teacher education budgets became defensive. As previously mentioned, many teacher education institutions had not paid enough attention to their student teaching program which was located "down the road" in the classrooms of K-12 school teachers. To ease their conscience concerning the haphazard method of "farming out" student teachers, college administrators consented to pay school districts and/or teachers for "helping out" with the preparation of teachers. The amount allocated for this was usually nominal and negotiation arithmetic showed it to be an embarrassing pittance. Battle lines were drawn and teacher education colleges were oftentimes coerced into higher stipends for supervising teachers and into developing more cooperative teacher education programs. Not all teacher education institutions and K–12 school districts fought the battle, but many did. Gradually, however, as the college teacher educators discussed the matter with their public and private school colleagues, it was determined that basically what the public school people desired was not necessarily money but a joint partnership in the teacher education process. After the classroom teacher's immediate concern for economic equality with comparable professions diminished, teachers through negotiations, looked into other professional matters which affected the total school environment. Three matters concerning teacher education about which classroom teachers felt strongly were:

(1) that individuals who had not been in an elementary-junior high-or high school classroom for years should not be teaching methods courses at teacher education colleges.

(2) that the practitioners themselves should be a part of the teacher education process.

(3) that the practitioners should be prepared by the colleges to do the job of supervising student teachers.

Concerning the latter, the colleges partially alleviated the problem by developing token in-service or pre-service programs designed to provide the supervising teacher with a degree of expertise in working with a student teacher. In addition, some colleges hired faculty members to work closely with the school districts to enhance communication and to help the student teachers have a successful experience. During the 1960's neither of these approaches were really effective. Colleges, not having enough money or incentive—or both—often did not provide adequate office facilities for this faculty member who resided off-campus and worked closely with public schools. Communication between campus and off-campus centers was often poor. Cooperating school personnel, still not completely understanding the relationship, often did not accept the off-campus staff member.

And so, the decade of the 1960's passed with the existence of the student teaching experience in the K-12 school environment in a very precarious situation.

SUMMARY

Although the education of man dates back to the very earliest of times, formal teacher education is comparatively new. Teacher education in the United States had its antecedents in Europe. During the nineteenth century the normal school opened and university education departments offered teacher education courses. An integral part of the course work was a practice teaching experience often located in a model school. As time progressed, however, most teacher education programs outgrew the model schools, or laboratory schools as they were later named, and expanded into neighboring communities for student teaching experiences. Unfortunately, a sound base for this initial relationship was not established and as the period of public school collective bargaining and labor negotiations came about, strained relationships occurred between the participating K-12 districts and teacher education colleges. These uneasy relationships would prevail during the 1960's and await the 1970's for solution.

CHAPTER TWO

Roles in Preparing Prospective Teachers in a Clinical Setting

Today, student teaching is entangled in a mass of confusion, unmade decisions, and expediencies. It lacks a comprehensive definition and a clear-cut statement of goals and purposes. Despite the fact that student teaching must be a cooperative endeavor, in many cases the personnel in colleges and universities, public schools, professional organizations, and state departments of education who are most concerned and involved are not working closely enough together. Some colleges and universities develop programs and merely notify the schools of their plans. Others turn the whole enterprise over to the public schools.

A New Order in Student Teaching: Fixing Responsibilities for Student Teaching. National Education Association, Washington, D.C., 1967.

Role of Professional Organizations

The above quotation from a publication of a professional education organization clearly illustrates the problems confronting teacher educators during the waning years of the 1960's. Cooperating classroom teachers and those college personnel directly involved with student teaching were thoroughly convinced that the student teaching situation was bad as early as 1960, but little concerted effort was mounted to alleviate the problem. Toward the end of the decade, however, various professional organizations exerted leadership directed toward the goal of establishing a true partnership between teacher education colleges and public and private schools involved in the student teaching experience.

One of the professional organizations which paved the way for more positive and successful partnerships was the Association for Student Teaching (AST),[1] an organization primarily for those classroom teachers and college personnel directly interested and involved in the student teaching experience. Through a series of workshops, clinics, and confer-

[1] This organization has changed its name to: The Association of Teacher Educators (ATE). The organization now includes membership from all areas of teacher education.

15

ences, the organization promoted partnership and greatly aided in defining the roles and responsibilities of each partner. Not only did the meetings contribute to improved partnership arrangements, but the results of the meetings were generally published for the participants as well as the total membership and other interested individuals. Particularly noteworthy was the 1968 publication entitled *Partnership in Teacher Education* which resulted from the 1966 summer workshop held on the campus of Indiana University of Pennsylvania. The focus of this workshop was directed toward the relationships of schools and colleges in providing laboratory experiences in teacher education.

In addition to this important workshop and resulting publication, the Association for Student Teaching, realizing the lack of role definitions in student teaching, made a concerted effort in the 1960's to aid the various personnel involved in student teaching to understand respective roles. Such publications as: *The College Supervisor* (1968), *The Director of Student Teaching* (1968), *Guiding Student Teaching Experiences* (1968), and *The Supervising Teacher, Standards for Selection and Function* and a host of other important publications contributed much to provide a better understanding of various aspects of teacher education and especially student teaching.

Two additional documents which helped to pave the way for successful partnerships during the early 1970's were the publications of the Joint Committee on State Responsibility for Student Teaching, a group appointed in 1964 by seven sponsoring agencies. The first publication was a discussion paper entitled, "Who's in Charge Here? Fixing Responsibilities for Student Teaching." These documents alerted individuals involved with the student teaching process to the seriousness of the problems inherent in student teaching and stimulated cooperative action between schools and colleges.

Also influential were the recommended standards for teacher education prepared by the Evaluative Criteria Study Committee and adopted by the Executive Committee of the American Association of Colleges for Teacher Education commonly known as NCATE (National Council for Accreditation of Teacher Education). These standards formed the basis for teacher education college accreditation in the early 1970's. The recommended standards emphasized clinical and student teaching experiences and motivated a great number of teacher education colleges to provide additional emphasis to this important area.

As the 1970's approached the previously mentioned factors caused loose college—school district liaisons to be somewhat tightened. More positive relationships were developing between various agencies involved in the student teaching aspect of teacher education. These partnership arrangements were based upon the assumption that prospective teachers cannot be adequately prepared without having access to a real environment in which to observe, participate, and teach. It is, therefore, well accepted today that if teacher education is to be viable then the K-12 school environment must be used extensively.

THE UNDERGRADUATE PREPARATION OF A TEACHER

Although the authors are primarily concerned with those roles dealing specifically with those working in student teaching, it is important to realize that many parts of the teacher education program are the result of work done on a college campus. To better understand the off-campus student teaching experience, and in order to establish a foundation for a satisfactory partnership in teacher education, it is necessary to understand the work that is performed on a college campus leading to initial teacher certification.

The Campus Based Teacher Education Program

Many studies have shown that the main reason individuals become teachers is because they enjoy working with school-age youth. This is an excellent reason and rightfully should rank highest of all. But there is much more than just the fact that one enjoys youth to enable one to become a successful teacher. A sound academic background is of the highest priority. Today, this usually means the acquisition of a series of courses leading to a major or minor sequence which provides depth in particular subject areas. In addition, there are those common learnings that are important to all in today's society and provide breadth of knowledge. These two segments: major and minor development and general education comprise the academic background of a prospective teacher.

In addition to academic preparation, there is a need to obtain knowledge of one's prospective profession, to gain knowledge about school-age youth, and to learn how to effectively translate this into a classroom environment. These sequences of collegiate courses are the foundational courses which involve the philosophical, historical, and sociological development of education, various child and adolescent psychology courses, and methods courses. In addition to these courses, pre-student teaching clinical experiences should be available to provide numerous opportunities to work with youth prior to any formal student teaching activity. These clinical experiences should be developed on a yearly sequential basis with the apex being the professional semester or student teaching experience.

Role of The Off-Campus Based Teacher Education Program

As previously mentioned, many teachers have regarded the student teaching experience to be the single most important aspect of a teacher education program. For decades, various education courses have been indicted for the lack of relevance, but seldom has the student teaching experience been so charged. Indictments have been made against sloppiness of the operation but not against the concept.

In the not-so-distant past, and unfortunately still dominant in some areas today, student teaching is synonymous with working with one classroom teacher, in one classroom, in one building, with one group of youngsters. This can result in tragedy if the supervising teacher happens to be poorly trained to supervise or serves as the single model. Today, forward looking educators are discarding this provincial student teaching plan and opening the total school environment to the prospective teacher. Modern laboratory experiences should follow four principles:

---

1. The Program for student teachers should provide great flexibility so that strengths and weaknesses of individual students will determine the specific program.

One of the frequent criticisms of present student teaching programs is the failure to provide for individual differences among students. Regardless of the maturity, academic aptitude, natural ability, or other personal factors involved, students usually have progressed through the same type of program, for the same length of time, with little attempt to design a student teaching experience around their particular strengths and weaknesses. This should not happen and a quality program for student teachers is one which allows the student to progress at his own rate of speed and provides as many varied experiences as possible during the allotted time period of the laboratory experience.

---

2. The Student Teacher should be involved in a program which is designed to provide contact with several teachers and various teaching styles.

This should alleviate the problem of limiting a student teacher to a particular style by modeling one supervising teacher. A well designed program should not be so narrowly structured. Instead, it should provide contact between the student teacher and several different classroom teachers, enabling him to learn from each as he seeks to develop his own teaching style.

---

3. The Program should be structured to provide many kinds of school experiences for the student teacher in addition to classroom teaching.

Student teachers need to participate in as many school activities as possible. Extracurricular activities are extremely important to students and should be to teachers. In addition, the program should be flexible enough to allow for visitations to various buildings and programs and to Board of Education meetings and the like. Every prospective elementary teacher should have planned visitations to secondary classrooms and vice versa. Too often a student teacher is scheduled to student teach full-time with a single teacher and is limited in the opportunity to participate in other activities which would be invaluable.

---

4. Effective means should be developed to bring practicing teachers and teacher preparation institutions into a true partnership in the design and implementation of teacher education programs.

Greater involvement by the classroom practitioners can facilitate the blending of the practical and the theoretical which can help teacher education programs be relevant to the needs of prospective teachers.[2]

ROLES WITHIN A COOPERATIVE TEACHER EDUCATION PROGRAM

The Promise of the 1970's

It is readily observed by educators that if teacher education in the 1970's is to be a meaningful experience, it must be a cooperative endeavor

[2] Dean, Leland, *Position Paper on Student Teaching Programs of Michigan Teacher Education Institutions.* Unpublished material.

between teacher educators at all levels. A true partnership arrangement with shared responsibilities in teacher education is mutually beneficial to teacher education institutions and cooperating school districts. The advantages to the college are rather obvious. They include the opportunity to provide prospective teachers with a practical experience:

(1) in a classroom teaching setting,
(2) in working with a variety of teachers and classroom specialists,
(3) in working with school administrators in administrative relationships, and
(4) in community living and community study.

These experiences, when analyzed through discussions and seminars with classroom teachers, administrators, other student teachers, and the college supervisor, enable the prospective teacher to become a better qualified first-year teacher.

The values of a partnership arrangement which accrue to the school system include:

(1) more highly individualized instruction for pupils as a result of the additional manpower in selected classrooms,
(2) professional and intellectual stimulation resulting from the presence of an enthusiastic college student teacher with recent training,
(3) released time for teachers to enable them to do curriculum work, visit other classrooms, and to attend in-service meetings to improve their teaching effectiveness.
(4) an advantageous method to select new faculty.

A Model

It would appear then that if a cooperative program is developed between the K-12 school districts and the college, the ingredients in such a model might include:

(1) joint participation in the development of teacher education programs between future teachers, practicing teachers, public school and private school administrators, and college personnel.
(2) joint K-12 school-college appointments whereby practitioners can participate in teaching methods courses, and in the supervision of student teaching and other clinical experiences.

(3) involvement of varied types of K-12 personnel in the off-campus program to enable student teachers to have access to a variety of experiences in the school environment.

(4) a college "open port" whereby cooperating school personnel would have total access to college facilities, including tuition refundable courses, for participating in the teacher education program.

(5) a K-12 school district "open port" whereby colleges would have total access to every building in the district to every room and to every teacher.

(6) colleges providing much more in-service help to those public and private school personnel who work closely with the teacher education program.

(7) college personnel involved in teacher education being familiar with what is happening in today's schools. In addition, teacher educators must realize that the best location for an individual to learn to become a teacher is in an elementary or secondary school, and not within the confines of a typical campus based college classroom situation.

(8) clinical experiences as a planned sequential program of activities, involving periods of the freshman, sophomore, junior, and senior years.

(9) the recognition by teacher associations, school district administrators, and state level governmental agencies that philosophically and functionally they must aid in the preparation of teachers.

Responsibilities of the College

With these points in mind, the tradition of institutions of higher education developing and implementing their own teacher education programs must be changed. The attitude that public and private schools are junior partners in teacher education can no longer be tolerated. A satisfactory full partnership must be developed. In such a partnership, each has definite responsibilities. The teacher preparation institutions must recognize as a primary responsibility the task of better preparing supervising teachers to work effectively with student teachers. A quality student teaching experience cannot be provided unless the supervisor with whom the student teacher is placed feels qualified and has a high degree of expertise in the supervision of student teachers. Not only should colleges prepare supervising teachers but also provide assistance to the cooperating school districts in the development and improvement of teaching at all levels. The total college resources must be available to improve education in all K-12 districts in which a cooperative teacher education program is developed. The colleges must also place high priority on the recognition of supervising teachers as professional colleagues, and, as much as possible, provide access to campus facilities and resources to the extent these facilities are available to the regular campus faculty.

Responsibilities of the Cooperating Schools

If the partnership is to fulfill all expectations, cooperating schools must recognize their responsibilities and philosophically accept their role in teacher preparation.

The cooperating schools can help by encouraging and participating in research related to teacher education and be open to innovations which promise to provide for continuous improvement of teaching. In addition, they should provide and encourage supervising teachers to participate in meetings, seminars and workshops related to student teaching and other types of clinical experiences. Cooperating schools should also be willing to accept students for clinical experiences *without* regard to the student's race, creed,· color, or sex. And hopefully, cooperating school systems in off-campus student teaching centers should provide the college supervisor with adequate office space, a suitable room for seminars, space for library materials and inter-school mailing services.

Teacher Education Councils

One method of ensuring that these basic obligations are met by both parties is the establishment of a Teacher Education Council. These councils have been very active and successful in many states and are often composed of supervising teachers, administrators, and college supervisors. The following teacher education council guidelines may be helpful in understanding the relationship of the council to school districts and colleges. The specific purposes and responsibilities of a teacher education council might be:

   (1) to encourage, help, or sponsor regional or area workshops designed to provide understanding and improved skills for those who work with student teachers,

   (2) to sponsor workshops and other in-service days for teachers in the K-12 districts by which college personnel would provide, free of charge, expertise in their areas of specialty.

(3) to develop an instrument and a process for evaluating the supervision of student teachers.

(4) to develop and support libraries and other teaching aids, which will facilitate not only the clinical experience for college students, but also provide first year teachers in the various districts with access to the materials.

(5) to administer all monetary affairs jointly.

(6) to design methods to provide feedback to the teacher education college from the K-12 environment concerning preparation of student teachers, and other concerns.

(7) to develop supervising teacher handbooks, student teacher handbooks, and other student teaching materials to insure that prospective supervising teachers and administrators have an understanding of the program and the responsibility involved.

(8) to develop and administer follow-up studies of graduates of the area's teacher education councils to provide information related to the value of the program.

(9) to provide flexible and individualized experiences for student teachers.

(10) to encourage an exchange of faculty between the teacher education institution and the K-12 district.

In general, then, the role and function of any teacher education council should be:

(1) to improve student teaching and teacher education,

(2) to serve in an advisory capacity to the colleges and to the districts involved,

(3) to serve as a clearinghouse for any recommendations concerning program or practices,

(4) to aid the cooperating school personnel to supervise student teachers, by providing materials and equipment to facilitate understanding.

These councils can be composed of representatives from many colleges and districts or from one college and many districts or from one college and one district, depending upon the amount of teacher education involvement in the area. Teacher Education Councils have proven to be extremely valuable contributors to the partnership arrangement and above all, have greatly enhanced communication between colleges and cooperating school districts.

PERSONNEL INVOLVED IN STUDENT TEACHING EXPERIENCES AND THEIR RESPECTIVE ROLES AND RESPONSIBILITIES

In any discussion of partnerships in teacher education, an understanding of the various important roles which individuals and groups have is necessary. These roles are important for all to understand and the failure to communicate and understand one another's roles is a major reason for a breakdown in any partnership arrangement.

Problem Situation #1

Student's Father to the Director of Student Teaching: I want Sally placed in Tech High School so she can live at home during her student teaching experience.

Student (Sally) to Director of Student Teaching: I want to be placed with Martha in Oil City. She's my roommate and we can live at her house.

College Band Director to Director of Student Teaching: I would appreciate it if every consideration could be given to Sally's staying on-campus to student teach so she can participate in the marching band.

Director of Student Teaching to himself: I guess I'll ask the Dean what to do.

College Roles in Partnership Programs

The Placement of student teachers is just one of the many roles of the *Director of Student Teaching.* His role is a vast and important one in the operation of the partnership. The Director of Student Teaching, or the person responsible for the operation of the student teaching program is the administrator charged with program leadership. Some of his more important responsibilities are:

(1) the maintainance of satisfactory public relations with the cooperating school districts.

(2) the development and administration of that portion of the university budget allocated to student teaching.

(3) the development and distribution of interpretative materials concerning student teaching for use by university supervisors and K-12 school district personnel.

(4) the development of various types of evaluation forms.

(5) the planning and staging of periodic meetings with students to prepare them for involvement in the various clinical experiences.

(6) the planning and hosting of workshops and conferences for cooperating K-12 administrators and teachers for in-service purposes.

(7) the coordination of off-campus orientation days whereby students, prior to their student teaching experience, have an opportunity to visit the environment where they will student teach.

(8) the periodic visitation of off-campus sites to meet with cooperating teachers and administrators and to visit students involved in clinical experiences.

(9) the placement of student teachers in a quality student teaching environment.

(10) the development and maintainance of university offices in the off-campus environment.

(11) the development, with cooperation from various on-campus and off-campus personnel, of realistic and individualized student teaching programs.

The college supervisor interprets the student teaching position to the student teachers and supervising teachers

(12) the development of student teaching agreements with various cooperating school districts.

As the reader will note, these responsibilities are extremely important and must be conscientiously performed to maintain a quality student teaching program.

Problem Situation #2

College Supervisor to the Director of Student Teaching: Why do I have 25 student teachers assigned to me? John has only 22 and fewer buildings to visit.

Director of Student Teaching: I know, but you only had 21 students last semester.

The College Supervisor

Certainly an important role of the college supervisor is visiting student teachers in the field and it is only natural to be concerned about the number of students assigned, yet the visitation of student teachers is only one aspect of the many roles of the college supervisor. For it is the college supervisor who has the important obligation of working directly with cooperating school personnel to provide realistic, relevant laboratory experiences for college students. This important role varies from college to college but can be classified into these categories. One is to work cooperatively with school personnel to provide high quality clinical experiences, the second is working effectively with student teachers in the clinical setting and the third can be classified as administrative responsibilities. A specific outline of responsibilities might be:

A. The College Supervisor works cooperatively with school personnel by:
   (1) providing pre-service and in-service experiences to administrators and supervising teachers and other school personnel with whom he works, to better prepare them to work effectively with college students.
   (2) honoring the cooperative personnel in various ways for services rendered.
   (3) interpreting teacher education programs.

(4) serving as a resource person, or consultant, when called upon.

(5) becoming an integral part of the school environment by availability at various school events, i.e., Board of Education meetings, P.T.A., athletic events, etc.

(6) Continuously evaluating the environment in which the student teacher is placed.

(7) being available to cooperating personnel and assisting and advising them concerning problems involving students in the clinical setting.

(8) visiting as often as possible the supervising teacher and administrator to discuss the progress of the student teacher. (The length and number of visitations should be based upon the needs of both the student teacher and the supervising teacher.)

(9) providing methods of evaluation feedback to the supervising teacher and the student teacher concerning the feelings of each.

(10) encouraging and promoting advisory councils for student teachers within a particular school district or center for the purpose of sharing policy decisions aimed at developing a true partnership relation in teacher education.

(11) maintaining up-to-date records regarding utilization of teachers, administrators, and resources which relate to the student teacher, and by maintaining and keeping up-to-date all policies relevant to the student teaching experience.

B. The College supervisor works effectively with student teachers by:

(1) securing quality student teaching placements.

(2) teaching courses designated by the School of Education as an integral part of the laboratory experience and by utilizing the full resources of local environments to promote a better relationship between theory and practice.

(3) visiting and observing the student teachers periodically to insure satisfactory progress on the part of the student teacher, and to effectively collaborate with the supervising teacher in the evaluation process.

(4) acting as a counselor and confidante to students.

(5) assisting students to secure housing.

(6) providing quality orientation experiences for the student.

(7) providing multi-faceted experiences during the professional

semester designed to enhance and promote the transition from student teacher to classroom teacher.

C. The college supervisor works cooperatively with the Student Teaching Office and the School of Education by:

    (1) making every effort to meet deadlines on required forms, schedules, placement lists, meetings, etc.

    (2) attending scheduled departmental meetings, conferences, and established committee meetings.

    (3) participating in professional organizations for personal and professional growth.

    (4) administering effectively the center budget or available monies.

In addition, college supervisors generally act as distributing centers for collegiate information, and, as such, provide services to many areas including the Admissions Office, Placement Office, Off-Campus Education Office, Athletic Office, Alumni Office, and the Registrar's Office.

Problem Situation #3

Principal—I haven't seen you around before. Are you substituting for Mr. Jones today?

Student Teacher—No, I'm Sally Smith, a student teacher. I've been working with Mr. Jones for the past six weeks.

Cooperating School Roles. The Building Administrator.

One of the most important roles and one of the least mentioned in the cooperative teacher education program is the role of the building administrator and his relationship to the program. If a cooperative teacher education program exists in a building, the principal should be very much involved. His involvement should include working closely with the college supervisor in placing the students in the school environment to enable students to have individualized and varied experiences. He must especially avoid placing a student with an overburdened, inefficient, or weak teacher. In addition the principal should make certain that the classroom teacher really desires to work with an observer, participator or student teacher. Above all, however, the principal needs to treat the student teacher as a faculty member. Student teachers are, in fact, extra professionals within a building, and, as such, should be given the same consideration which a teacher receives. It would appear then that the principal would need to make the student teacher welcome, that he would need to give them some status within the building by providing the student teacher with a mailbox, desk, and other materials to enhance the student teacher's chances of being successful, and that he should try in every way to interpret school policies to the student teacher just as he would to a new fledgling teacher. This responsibility could be met by providing a tour of the building, an orientation to building operational procedures, and, if available, a faculty handbook for the student teacher. In addition, the building administrator has the responsibility for encouraging outstanding classroom teachers to become supervisors. The principal should also work closely with the college supervisor to provide in-service experiences for supervising teachers to better enable them to work successfully with student teachers. He should also protect student teachers from undue burdens placed on them by supervising teachers and insure that the supervising teacher is fulfilling his role. All in all, the building principal has a very important role in the cooperative teacher education program and one that unfortunately is often performed inadequately.

Problem Situation #4

Special Education Supervising teacher—Class, how do you like your student teacher, Miss Jones?

Johnny in the fourth row—Oh, we like her, she's more like us!

The Role of the Supervising Teacher

The supervising teacher is the individual who works closely with the student teacher in the classroom and has one of the most critical roles in the teacher education process. Certainly, as the above problem situation indicates, one of the important responsibilities of the supervising teacher is to provide an atmosphere whereby the student teacher is accepted by the students.

Various studies indicate that the single most important individual in the student teaching process is the supervising teacher. It is this person who daily interacts with teacher education students and provides the classroom environment so necessary for a satisfying clinical experience. Teachers are generally designated as supervising teachers by the school system and the teacher education colleges on a cooperative basis and the selection process usually requires:

(1) that the prospective supervising teacher meet the education and certification standards established by the college or state which usually requests that the supervising teacher be certified and have a baccalaureate degree or preferably, a master's degree.

(2) that the supervising teacher has exemplified certain professional competencies, has effective interpersonal relations and is classified as a highly competent teacher,

(3) that the supervising teacher indicate an interest in having a student teacher and being involved in a cooperative teacher education program.

With these characteristics in mind, it is important to understand the multiple responsibilities of the supervising teacher. The responsibilities of the supervising teacher usually include:

(1) Planning for the initial orientation of the student teacher to the classroom.

(2) Acquainting himself with the program of teacher education and student teaching as proposed and developed cooperatively by the college and the school district.

(3) Familiarizing himself with the background of the student teacher through materials obtained from the college.

(4) Creating an atmosphere of acceptance for the student on the part of himself, the pupils, the faculty and the community.

(5) Introducing the student teacher to classroom routines and instructional procedures.

(6) Providing observational and participatory opportunities for the student teacher in various class and extra-class activities.

(7) Acquainting the student teacher with pupil personnel records and the manner in which they are maintained and used.

(8) Acquainting the student teacher with available instructional materials, supplies, and equipment.

(9) Orienting the student teacher to the accepted pattern of planning.

(10) Establishing a climate in which the student teacher may

gradually develop skills in planning and continuously evaluate his own planning procedures.

(11) Treating the student teacher as a co-worker, rather than as a subordinate.

(12) Providing opportunities for the student teacher to test theory and practice in a variety of classroom and extra-class situations.

(13) Arranging the schedule for actual teaching experiences by the student teacher.

(14) Providing for continuous evaluation of the student's teaching through frequent planned conferences; weekly report sheets; self-evaluation by the student teacher; check-lists, and through final evaluation procedures.

(15) Helping the student teacher establish objectives.

(16) Providing the student teacher opportunities for professional growth by encouraging attendance at professional meetings.

(17) Providing opportunities for conferences with the student teacher.

Noting these responsibilities, it is important to emphasize some of the more critical. The supervising teacher, to be truly effective, must accept the student teacher as an associate or colleague, and, remember that the student teacher is a novice and therefore needs a great deal of orientation and introduction to the classroom, school building and community. A helpful hint to all supervising teachers is the importance of conveying early to the student teacher particular likes and dislikes, procedures which should be used, and procedures which should not be used. A student teacher must know the ground rules to be effective, and few supervising teachers have the same operating procedures, so it is the obligation of the supervising teacher to tell the student teacher the accepted policies and procedures. The supervising teacher must exemplify good teaching techniques for they are in a "fishbowl" situation. Oftentimes this is the first classroom teacher that the student teacher has seen perform since high school days. The supervising teacher as a model has a tremendous influence on a fledgling teacher.

Perhaps the most difficult of all the roles for the supervising teacher to perform is that of relinquishing classroom responsibility to the neophyte. This responsibility, however, must be met if the student teacher is to develop a repertoire of teaching techniques and if the student is to be aware of teaching strengths and weaknesses.

Another extremely difficult role for the supervising teacher to perform is that of evaluation. If there is one persistent criticism of the supervising teacher, it is that he did not evaluate the student teacher enough. The supervising teacher must evaluate the student teacher on a continuous basis for the student teacher needs to be evaluated and to understand the evaluation. On all evaluations, the supervising teacher must be critical and yet fair. The authors feel that evaluation is so extremely important that a chapter has been devoted to this topic.

Problem Situation #5

Director of Student Teaching to prospective student teachers: Remember, the public school environment is much different than here at the college.

Prospective student teacher—Does that mean my beard and bib overalls have to go?

The Role of the Student Teacher

Although the supervising teacher assumes the major responsibility for directing the student teacher in his work, the student teacher has important responsibilities if he is to derive full benefit from the student teaching experience. Above all, the student teacher should be enthusiastic and interested in becoming a teacher. The student teacher should also be prepared to guide the learning experiences of youngsters and to translate learnings gathered on a college campus into a classroom.

One can expect the student teacher to be well prepared to teach. Student teachers are usually seniors in college with approximately three and a half years of general education and major and minor coursework. Student teachers should also have taken the proper and necessary professional education courses designed to provide an understanding of the age group with which the student wishes to work, the historical and philosophical background of the private, and public school, and the necessary techniques needed to operate audio and visual teaching aides. Of course, the effective translating of these courses into the classroom is what student teaching is all about—but the supervising teacher can, and should, expect eager, enthusiastic, well prepared student teachers. To settle for less is performing a disservice to the profession. Other specific responsibilities of the student teacher include:

(1) Providing his supervising teacher with pertinent background information.

(2) Conducting himself in a manner befitting his position in the

school and conforming to the mores and customs, such as dress, speech, and personal habits, found in the school and community.

(3) Notifying the supervising teacher, school principal, the area coordinator, and/or the college supervisor of any absences or contemplated change in the student teaching schedule.

(4) Refraining from discussion of confidential information.

(5) Becoming acquainted with school personnel and their functions.

(6) Assisting in housekeeping duties, routine procedures, and co-curricular activities.

(7) Taking the initiative in seeking help from the supervising teacher.

(8) Acquiring pertinent information about pupils for whom he is responsible and becoming acquainted with them.

(9) Gaining information about long-range and unit plans in current use, and developing daily and unit plans for teaching with the help and guidance of the supervising teacher.

(10) Attending school functions such as P.T.A. meetings, faculty meetings, and other events that teachers normally are expected to attend.

(11) Attending seminars, conferences, and workshops scheduled by the school or the college.

(12) Continuing the development of a professional attitude.

(13) Keeping the college supervisor informed of progress made and problems encountered.

(14) Learning and carrying out school policies and procedures.[3]

All of the previously mentioned roles are extremely important to the success of a student teacher and each must be understood by the various other parties involved in the teacher education process.

An understanding of the various roles in the cooperative teacher education program is needed but equally important, is for colleges and school districts to share in the development of a cooperative agreement concerning working procedures. A clearly outlined description of procedures for school personnel who work with teacher education programs on a cooperative basis is taken from the Waterford, Michigan Township District.

[3] *A Handbook for Student Teaching*—School of Education, Indiana University, Bloomington, Indiana. 1973—p. 7.

Figure 2-1

The Waterford Township Administrative Procedural Statement concerning student teachers and student observers

The Waterford Township School District perceives the roles as:

A. Assistant Superintendent for General Administration shall be the Central Office administrator in charge of student teachers and student observer programs that operate within the School District. Specifically, the responsibilities of the Assistant Superintendent for General Administration are:

  (1) To meet with the student teachers and present general information about the School District by—
      a. Indicating an interest in quality teachers,
      b. Defining areas of opportunity for new teachers,
      c. Distributing teacher recruitment materials,
      d. Extending a warm invitation to student teach in the Waterford District and possibly to eventually teach in the Waterford School District.

  (2) To work closely with college supervisors to identify those students who present good potential as prospective teachers.

  (3) To participate as a full partner in the teacher education process by making recommendations which positively affect the teacher education program. In addition, whenever practical, meet with supervising teachers to help them understand and perform their role more capably.

  (4) To indicate a warm reception to the Waterford School District to visiting students either by direct contact or by personal letter.

B. The Elementary Coordinator or Secondary Coordinator shall have the responsibility for the supervision of student teachers and observers who are assigned to his instructional areas. He shall work cooperatively with the representative of the teacher education institution, the building principals, and the supervising teacher in the selection, placement and supervision of student observers and student teachers. When an arrangement has been made for the placing of a student teacher or observer, the respective coordinator will report the person's name to the Assistant Superintendent for General Administration.

C. The Building Principal shall have the responsibility for working cooperatively with either the elementary or secondary coordinator, the representative of the teacher education institution, and the building teaching staff in the placement of student teachers and observers. The principal is responsible for the supervision and direction of student teachers or observers to the extent that it is necessary for him to carry out his responsibility as chief administrative officer for the building.

D. The Supervising Teacher shall be responsible for all aspects of the student teachers' activities while he is in the building. The supervising teacher has direct supervisory responsibility for the student teacher, and should insure that as much practical classroom experience as possible is gained. The supervising teacher will involve the student teacher in as much of the instructional process as is consistent with good teaching procedure. It is emphasized that the presence of a student teacher does not alter the responsibility of a classroom teacher for the instruction of students under his jurisdiction. The supervising teacher must assume full responsibility for the instruction provided by the student teacher and take any action necessary to insure an instructional program is conducted at high level.

The Waterford School District also believes that the teacher education institutions have a definite responsibility and mentions that:

A. The representative of the teacher education institution is responsible for working cooperatively with the coordinator, the principal, and the supervising teacher in the placement and supervision of student teachers and observers.

B. The teacher education institution should screen candidates so that student teachers will arrive with a seriousness of intent, and proper orientation for teaching.

C. The teacher education institution will provide orientation and guidance for both student teacher and supervising teacher prior to and during the term of student teaching.

D. The teacher education institution will provide funds to the Waterford School District as agreed.

E. The teacher education institution will work within the operating guidelines of the Waterford School District.

Of particular interest in the Waterford District's outline of responsibility is the fact that one office has been designated as the office responsible for the cooperative teacher education program in the district. This concept contributes to improved communications.

A SCHOOL DISTRICT INITIATES A COOPERATIVE TEACHER EDUCATION AGREEMENT

A Unique Development in Cooperative Teacher Education

One of the most promising developments in the growth of cooperative teacher education programs is the relatively unique situation whereby a school district initiates and develops a cooperative teacher education program with a college. Historically, colleges have approached school districts with requests to place student teachers or observers in the district. The Bay City Bangor School District in Michigan, however, is one district that realized the advantages of a student teaching program in its district and in its agreement of such items as length of experience, type of experience, advantages of the program to student teachers as well as to the School District. Of particular interest are the advantages which the school district feels it will derive from such an association. They are:

1. The close association with the university, which we want and need.
2. The up-grading of education by helping students become aware of what school can be like.
3. The development of a pool of available teachers for recruiting purposes—teachers who are well known to us.
4. The involvement of our teachers in seminars for continuing education.
5. The growth on the part of the professional staff. Supervising teachers and independent study supervisors will encourage the student teacher to put his ideas into action. We will learn and grow as much as the student teachers.
6. The contact with fresh, vital creative young people just entering the profession.
7. The development of a laboratory school in our off-campus center which would be a model for other schools in the area.
8. The belief that through such a cooperative program that our students would get a superior education because of extra staff, and the freshness of new and innovative ideas from recently college-educated youth.

This is an excellent example of the cooperative relationship between a college and a school district. Of special interest is the fact that this school district is willing to share its educational resources to help prepare future teachers. To teacher educators, however, more important is the fact that this school district has realized the importance of having student teachers and the contributions which will be made to the teachers, to the Bangor students, and to the community.

A true partnership in teacher education exists when both parties respect one another and both realize the importance and value of mutual cooperation.

SUMMARY

It was realized, during the waning years of the 1960's that if quality laboratory experiences were to exist, a true partnership between colleges and public schools needed to emerge; a partnership which would be equal and which would be designed for the benefit of all concerned. During the early years of the 1970's many such partnerships developed. Colleges realized that quality undergraduate teacher education programs could not exist without the full cooperation of the school districts. Many cooperating school districts also realized the mutual advantages of participating in a teacher education program. Off-campus teacher education centers were developed, full-time faculty members were assigned to work with student teachers in the centers, attention was given to the pre-service and in-service preparation of supervising teachers, teacher education councils developed and the roles of individuals participating in the partnership were defined. In addition, school district teachers and administrators shared in decisions affecting professional education and contributed to the increasing relevancy of professional education courses by actual participation in the teaching of the courses. All in all, the decade of the 1970's promises to bring the school district-teacher education college relationship even closer.

CHAPTER THREE

Toward a Theory of Student Teaching Supervision

Practice must be based upon logical theory.

One of the often neglected subjects related to student teaching supervision is that dealing with the theory of this field. In fact, it is unfortunately true that relatively little has been written on this extremely important topic. There is, however, an increasing interest throughout teacher education in this topic.

In a recent study[1] a theoretical structure was suggested for clinical experiences in teacher education (early in-classroom exposure of teacher trainees; microteaching; simulation; and student teaching), based on Abraham Maslow's theory of motivation. In this chapter implications of Maslow's theory will be outlined in the specific context of the supervising teacher—that role indicated by a large (and growing) body of research to be the most influential supervisory role in the student teaching experience.

The primary questions to be addressed here are these:

1. What are the goals of the student teaching experience? What is student teaching supposed to accomplish?
2. What does research have to say about the degree to which student teaching has met its goals?
3. How can a knowledge of Maslow's theory of motivation assist a supervising teacher in carrying out his vital role toward helping the student teacher attain the goals of student teaching?

Goals of Student Teaching.

Much has been written concerning the goals (or objectives) of the student teaching experience. Dussault[2] reviewed the literature on student

[1] This study was conducted by Dr. Alan Warner, now at the University of Houston. We thank Dr. Warner for the material presented in this chapter.

[2] Dussault, G. *A Theory of Supervision in Teacher Education.* New York: Teachers College Press, 1970.

teaching and other professional laboratory experiences from 1931 to 1968, and listed forty-five general goals derived from that literature. Each of these goals, if this were to be an exercise in behavioral objective writing, could be broken down into a score or more of constituent objectives.

But taken together, these goals present a picture something like this. The type of product that teacher educators hope to produce is a beginning teacher who enjoys working with pupils, finds great satisfaction in helping them learn; who possesses the necessary skills to accomplish this end; and who is open to new ideas and experiences so that she can grow in the teaching profession.

This goal is virtually identical with a construct that Abrahm Maslow calls the *self-actualized* person, operating in a synergic environment. Maslow's self-actualized person is realizing his or her fullest potential, becoming the best that he or she can become. By a synergic environment, Maslow means an environment in which the needs of the individual and the needs of those with whom he or she associates are together satisfied by the mutual relationship.

According to Maslow[3,4,5] almost everyone is born with a *need* for self-actualization, an instinctive desire to become the best that one can become. But one is also born with *other* needs that are *stronger* than the need for self-actualization, and that these must be gratified before one is even concerned about becoming self-actualized. These more powerful needs are: physiological; safety; love and belongingness; and esteem.

Attitudinal Changes as a Result of Student Teaching.

How well does the student teaching experience accomplish the goal stated above? Or put another way, how well does the student teaching experience succeed in gratifying needs that are *stronger* than the need for self-actualization, so that the neophyte teacher can progress toward a level of self-actualization in the teaching role? What does attitudinal research have to say about how student teachers are oriented when they *begin* the student teaching experience, and how they are oriented

[3] Maslow, A. H. *Toward a Psychology of Being.* (2nd ed.) New York: Van Nostrand Reinhold, 1968.

[4] Maslow, A. H. *Motivation and Personality.* (2nd ed.) New York: Harper & Row, 1970.

[5] Maslow, A. H. *The Farther Reaches of Human Nature.* New York: Viking Press, 1971

at the *completion* of that experience?

Aspy[6] reviewed a number of studies concerning anxieties expressed during teacher training and during the initial years of teaching. He concluded:

> . . . the majority of our student teachers are operating in fear as they enter their final phase of teacher training. According to Maslow, they would be operating at the safety level, which means they are concerned with their own survival at a time when we are asking them to give to others.

Dussault, in his review of the literature mentioned earlier, reviewed studies from 1931 to 1968 which utilized professional laboratory experiences (almost exclusively student teaching) as the independent variable and attitude changes on the part of teacher trainees as the dependent variable. By scanning his review, one reaches several apparent conclusions. The first is that a considerable number of questions remain to be investigated related to objectives and outcomes of student teaching. The second conclusion is that a number of the relations between objectives and outcomes are not sufficiently directional to indicate success or failure in attaining these objectives. The third conclusion is that, among those research findings which *do* indicate a definite direction, like the proverbial Indian chief they bear both good news and bad news.

Problem Situation #6

Bill is scheduled to do his student teaching in a junior high school next semester and has requested permission to keep his part-time bartending job while student teaching. He claims it is a financial must. Would you give him permission to do so? Why?

Changes in a positive direction include:

—positive changes in self-concept
—greater acceptance of others
—greater reality-orientation
—less self-depreciation
—improvement in teaching skills

[6]Aspy, D. N. Maslow and teachers in training. *Journal of Teacher Education,* 1969, Vol. 20, PP. 304–309.

—improved ability to work with children
—better understanding of children
—greater self-autonomy and decision-making
—greater correlation between perceptions of ideal and actual own teaching role
—more positive perceptions of ideal and actual teachers
—decrease in professional anxieties

Assuming that the desired outcome of student teaching is a teacher who enjoys working with students, who is open to new ideas and approaches, who begins to develop her own personal idiosyncratic teaching, and so on, the "bad news" effects of student teaching are:

—less openness to experience
—adoption of accepted practices
—adoption of supervising teacher's methods of teaching
—adoption of supervising teacher's methods of classroom housekeeping
—less logical consistency of ideas about education
—more negative perception of child behavior
—more custodial pupil-control ideology

Sorenson and Halpert[7] found that 70 per cent of the student teachers whom they studied experienced "considerable psychological discomfort" at the beginning of the student teaching experience, and 20 per cent carried that discomfort with them to the end of the assignment. The researchers identified five stress factors. Two of these dealt with the *nature* of discomfort: physical discomfort and irritability, and feelings of personal inadequacy and uncertainty about the teaching role. Two more factors were identified as *sources* of discomfort: disagreements between the student teacher and the supervising teacher concerning teaching practices, and perceived differences in personality between student teacher and supervising teacher.

The fifth factor which Sorenson and Halpert identified concerned the relationships between the student teacher and pupils. The researchers were unsure whether to assign this variable to either source of discomfort, or a nature (or type) of discomfort. They refer to this scale as "dislike of students."

Do the results of research given above support Aspy's charge that teacher trainees are operating at a *safety* level of behavior during the final phase of their training?

[7] Sorenson, G. & Halpert. R. Stress in student teaching. *Readings in Student Teaching for those who Work with Student Teachers.* (2nd ed.) Eds. J. A. Johnson & F. Perry. Dubuque, Iowa: Kendall-Hunt, 1969, pp. 367–373.

Answering this question requires, first of all, operationalizing the term "safety" in this specific context. What constitutes safety here? What is the goal of the organism (in this case, the student teacher)?

Student teaching is usually a terminal experience in a teacher education program. The student teacher is often in the final semester of his undergraduate college career. What is his most immediate goal? To graduate. To complete the program. In order to complete his college career, he must complete student teaching. The diploma constitutes the consummation of sixteen years of schooling. It represents a considerable amount of effort and the allocation of numerous resources. Reaching that goal constitutes immediate perceived safety.

It is not surprising then that the student teacher should model a considerable amount of his classroom teaching behavior after that of the supervising teacher—that the supervising teacher becomes a "significant other" to the point where disagreements between the student teacher and supervisor tend to result in, as Sorenson and Halpert phrase it, "considerable psychological discomfort" on the part of the student teacher.

What of the pupils in the student teacher's charge? The supervising teacher, the university supervisor, and the entire educational staff back at the University want the student teacher to like the children he is teaching, to help those children learn, to show respect for their abilities.

But the student teacher sees a necessity of presenting himself to his evaluators as poised, confident, in control of his classes. This type of image, after all, is vital to success.

The students don't quite understand. With a new person in charge of the class, the rules change. The children test, probe, explore this new leader to determine the limits he will place on their behavior. And the novice teacher views this pupil behavior as a threat to reaching the goal that is so close after so many years, the diploma.

It is to be expected that, upon completing this stressful experience, the positive changes in attitude identified by Dussault would also follow. Having successfully completed the student teaching experience with all its strains, it is to be expected that the student teacher will feel better about himself. He has, after all, adopted many of his supervising teacher's methods in order to succeed.

Almost everyone does succeed in student teaching. Johnson[8] found that 86 percent of responding institutions on his survey reported failing one percent or less of their student teachers on the first assignment. But in succeeding, some less than desirable attitudes have been fostered.

[8] Johnson, J. A. *A National Survey of Student Teaching Programs.* Baltimore: Multi-State Teacher Education Project, 1968.

An example of a student teacher helping children to teach.

One intention (or objective) was for the student teacher to use the skills gained in earlier training, to test them, to use them in developing his own idiosyncratic teaching style. But instead, he simply adopted many of the methods of his supervising teacher—who had adopted many of those of *his* supervising teacher. The *status quo* lives.

Problem Situation: 7

Sue is doing her student teaching in a sixth grade and has already signed a contract to teach in a small school next year. She has done so poorly in her student teaching that her college supervisor feels she should fail. What do you as the supervising teacher think?

Another objective was to open the student teacher's mind to experience. The stresses of the situation have instead made his mind *less* open.

The student teacher was supposed to develop a fairly rational philosophy concerning education and his own teaching. He was so busy meeting everyone's expectations, however, that he had little time to attempt to synthesize the theory he had been taught on campus with the practices he was expected to display in the classroom. He ended the experience with *less* logical consistency of his ideas about education than when he began.

The trainee was supposed to learn to like the age-group of children he was preparing to teach as a career. But with all the other stresses, all the other expectations he had to meet, the pupils really got in the way. They, after all, were not the ones to make the final evaluation. And much of the final evaluation rested on how well he controlled or "guided" them. The pupils' attempts to determine the "new rules" with the new leader were not perceived as a natural phenomenon but rather a threat to success, to safety. And finally, under the stresses of the situation, the trainee began to question whether teaching was *really* the type of career to which he would like to devote his life. But this was the last semester of the senior year! It was much too late to change. So he made it through, he did what was expected, he got the degree. Then perhaps he took a teaching job, and perhaps for just a year or two until he found something more exciting, more personality fulfilling.

The reader at this point may feel that an overly dismal picture of student teaching is being painted. But the previous discussion did not wander from the findings summarized by Dussault, those of Sorenson and Halpert, and an additional, consistent research finding—that 50 percent of the people who enter teaching do not stay in teaching longer than ten years.

The question remains: Does student teaching have to be this way? As least one study suggests that it does not. Fuller, Pilgrim and Freeland[9] reported the results of an experiment which involved providing counseling and close supervision to student teachers. The researchers identified six developmental stages during the student teaching experience.

In the first stage, trainees were concerned about the question, "Where do I stand?" This initial stage concerned placements, school rules, identifying and ascertaining the expectations of various supervisory personnel.

The second stage involved concerns about the student teachers'

[9]Fuller, F. F., Pilgrim, G. H., and Freeland, A. M. Intensive Individualization of Teacher Preparation. *Mental Health and Teacher Education.* 46th Yearbook, Association for Student Teaching. Dubuque, Iowa: Wm. C. Brown, 1967.

perceptions of their adequacy in the teaching role. Anxieties about subject-matter adequacy and class control were highly evident.

A desire to determine the causes of deviant behavior on the part of students was evidenced in the third stage, while the fourth stage exhibited a desire for evaluation, for feedback, from supervisors, parents, principals, and other teachers. In the fifth stage, trainees began to display a concern for what their pupils were *learning* as opposed to what they were being *taught*. Finally, student teachers reflected a full concern for their pupils and began to achieve new understandings of themselves through their relationships with pupils.

Two points need to be made with regards to this study. The first is that these developmental stages parallel rather nicely the sequence of Maslow's theory of motivation, or at least the intermediate stages (safety, love and belongingness, esteem). The first two stages obviously fit quite well into ego-centered safety concerns. Stages three through five exhibit a movement from safety to belongingness, from ego-centered concerns to concerns about others. And the final stage shows the beginnings of a synergic environment—one in which the needs of the individual (in this case, the teacher trainee) and the needs of those about him are together being satisfied by the mutual relationship.

The second point to be made concerning this study is that few schools of education exist that can afford such close supervision and counseling on a regular basis with their student teachers. The results of the research summarized by Dussault, and the study by Sorenson and Halpert, suggest that most student teachers do not advance beyond the *fourth* developmental stage: concerns for feedback, for evaluation.

The Supervising Teacher.

What part can the supervising teacher play in improving the student teaching experience from this analysis? Perhaps the most productive way of organizing some suggestions would be to address each of the needs that Maslow says are stronger than the need for self-actualization, one by one. Assuming that physiological needs are relatively well gratified (that is, the student teacher is not driven by hunger, thirst, and so on)—how can safety, love and belongingness, and esteem needs be addressed?

One way of assuring safety to the student teacher, of course, would be to assure him that he would not fail the student teaching experience. But the supervising teacher has an evaluative function. He has a responsibility to the profession, and to children perhaps as yet unborn, to see that incompetent teachers are not summarily ushered into the classroom.

Maslow, however, often uses the term safety almost synonymously with the term *stability*. People tend to react defensively in an environment that is too unpredictable, that changes without warning—where expectations are not clear and known. What expectations does the supervising teacher have of the student teacher? And what does he expect of him in return? These questions should be addressed at the outset of the experience. Are lesson plans to be prepared? How often will formal evaluation conferences be held? What will be the basis for evaluation? How much time will be spent in observation? Mutual planning? Tutoring or working with small groups?

According to Fuller, et. al., the first question that student teachers express center around, "Where do I stand?" These questions are concerned with safety and stability, and should be addressed immediately.

To what groups should the student teacher be helped to feel that he *belongs?* Certainly, he should be assisted in feeling part of the profession by the end of the student teaching experience. And research suggests that student teaching is relatively successful in this respect. If modelling of teaching behavior is any indication, he identified rather closely with the supervising teacher. And his perceptions of teachers in the field are more positive at the end of the student teaching experience than they were at the beginning.

But what about his perception of pupils? Research suggests that his views of pupils are more *negative* after student teaching. This is an unfortunate finding.

Problem Situation: #8

Jim, a student teacher in a high school history class is bitterly disappointed because the unit he has enthusiastically planned is failing to interest the class. Many of the students appear bored. What suggestions might you have for him?

A student may decide to become a teacher because of past experiences with exceptional teachers. A student may enter the profession because of positive relationships with teachers with whom he works, but he certainly does not stay in teaching very long simply for the opportunity to socialize with other teachers. If a new teacher does not like children and is not attracted to the everyday tasks of helping them learn, he is not going to remain a teacher very long (by his own choice or that of others).

An apparent necessity exists, then, to give the student teacher opportunities early in the experience to work with individual pupils and small groups before thrusting him before an entire class. Through such activities he can develop positive relationships with pupils much more easily than is possible when trying to control the dynamics of twenty, thirty, or more pupils. In working with individuals or small groups the individuality of pupils becomes much more apparent, and more attractive.

Esteem needs, according to Maslow, are broken down into two subsidiary sets: self-esteem, and esteem from others. The two are by no means exclusive—they must exist together. Moreover, the more self-esteem one has, the greater the ability to deal with failure.

The implications for student teaching should be obvious. Initial activities in the student teaching experience should be relatively simple, guaranteeing success (as much, of course, as anything in life can be guaranteed). As the activities become more complex, past successes become building blocks in confidence for the student teacher. A typical sequence might include: individual tutoring; leading small group discussions; splitting classes in half between the student teacher and supervising teacher; the student teacher handling full classes occasionally; and finally, the student teacher having full responsibility for entire classes.

Feedback, of course, is important to esteem. If the student teacher has done a good job in a particular instance, he should be told so by the supervising teacher. If an activity is not so successful (or a total flop) the student teacher will be much more able to deal with that failure if he rests on a series of other successes.

SUMMARY

According to almost everything that is known about student teaching, the one individual that makes—or breaks—that experience for the student teacher is the supervising teacher. At least as much as anyone else in the teacher education program, the supervising teacher by his actions determines whether the student teacher with whom he works finds teaching to be a role that is rewarding as a career; a role in which he can grow. The teaching profession sorely needs new teachers who are so oriented.

CHAPTER FOUR

Communications Techniques

Problem Situation #9

Principals:	What do they mean, my teachers need an in-service program in supervision?
Directors of Field Experiences:	I can't understand why they never give us the same supervising teacher for consecutive student teachers.
Student Teachers:	I thought I was doing what she wanted.
Supervising Teachers:	Why can't the college supervisor realize that this isn't a laboratory school?
College Supervisors:	Why is it that our supervisory team always seems to be two against one—the student and supervising teacher against me?

Problems? They certainly are, but how many are real and how many represent the inability of people to communicate with each other? All of us know what we mean, but how often or by what means do we insure that others know or accept the same meaning? All teachers are involved with the communication process, but how many have given it much thought; much less studied it? Even if we have, most of our thought and study has been related to communication between a teacher (me) and my pupils (them). The student teacher-supervising teacher relationship does exemplify many of the "me" and "them" characteristics; but if it is to operate at the highest professional levels, it must also include a peer communication relationship. This level of communication must obviously operate between the other partners also—administrators, teachers, directors, supervisors; but how frequently is communication with peers attempted at anything beyond the pleasantries level? This chapter does not purport to offer all solutions, but rather places its major emphasis upon an awareness of the importance of communication and providing some means for improvement. The real solutions lie with you and your determination to improve your understanding of others and theirs of you.

CHARACTERISTICS OF POSITIVE COMMUNICATION

The development of field experience programs as described in the first two chapters is replete with instances of injured feelings and noble improvement efforts that either failed completely or were less successful than intended because the parties involved simply did not understand or completely accept the roles and responsibilities assigned to them. The partnership movement, too, has been slow to develop because communication has been primarily a one-way street from the colleges to the schools. Negative communication is a stumbling block at the program level as well as the personal level. Many people use forms of negative communication with little awareness of doing it or of the consequences produced. A recognition of some of the more common types of negative communication may provide a basis for better understanding and acceptance of the principles of positive communication. This is attempted in Figure 4:1. The reader is invited to add some of his own favorites in the spaces provided.

Figure 4:1 Communication—What It's Not

Positive communication is not—

—the squack and squeal from the public address system.

—the memo addressed "Dear Parents" that the students throw away

—the yellowed bulletin board pronouncement.

—the personal letter from the college addressed "Dear Supervising Teacher."

—the slam of the classroom door following a discipline conference.

—the supervising teacher's comment, "It's not the way I would have done it."

—the student teacher who says, "Now I know what she meant."

—

—

All of the examples in Figure 4:1 communicate, and most people have uncomfortable feelings about these types. Something about them irritates and instead of accomplishing their intended communication objective they usually produce opposite effects. All parties to the teacher-educator mission might well consider that good communication is necessary and will happen best when it is consciously attempted. The characteristics which follow are hardly unique. Attention to them, however, might help all of us communicate more adequately.

Purposeful.

Positive communication must have an intent clear to all parties involved. This does not mean positive communication must be limited only to those items which concern "all business" or only to those situations where the supervisor has "something to say,"; but rather that the recipient be able to detect clearly the purpose of the communication. Purpose must characterize all communication, observation, and planning. All of us have at times been party to communication by riddle, planning that has had as much accident as purpose, and engaged in observations that may have been meaningful but incidental. Effective supervision, however, has a clearly stated purpose. The knowledge of intent is as important to consider when communicating as it is in lesson planning and observation. One of the simplest ways to insure that purpose is understood when communicating is to state the purpose openly. One need not classify every intent, but it does mean that care must be taken not to infuse a variety of purposes within a single communication act. Thus, a cheery, "Good morning," followed by, "How nice you look today," which is followed by, "Your college supervisor called last night to say that he will be here today," and "I hope you will make a better impression than you did when he last visited," and which continues with, "Your plans for today looked just beautiful last night, but they will need some last minute changes," and concludes with, "You seem in such a good mood, I almost hesitate to upset you before he arrives.", is apt to leave the student teacher more than a little mystified about the intent of the communication.

It is not uncommon to find supervising teachers hesitant to communicate their true feelings to their student teachers. It is likewise not uncommon that this inability on the part of the supervising teacher is one of the major criticisms by student teachers. If this represents the point of view of the two most important parties to the supervisory act, then it seems only logical that clearly establishing purpose for communication is one of the major ways to insure that positive communications take place.

Problem Situation #10

During the instructional observation on his third visit, the college supervisor notes that the student teacher obviously does not know all of his pupils by name. In the post-observation conference, he further perceives that the student and supervising teacher tend to refer to students by their location in the room.

Personalized.

Few of us care for communications which classify us in some generalized fashion Our personal identities are important and significance is attached to those situations and persons who give positive indication that they hold the same viewpoint. A concerned teacher preparation institution will take great pains to provide both the college supervisor and supervising teacher with as much personal background information about the teacher education student as possible. This serves the dual purpose of furnishing the supervising teacher with sufficient background information about the student so that he can make an informed decision with respect to working with that student, and also provides a starting point for insuring positive communication. One of the very first personalized supervisory activities should be an attempt to become as familiar as possible with the student, his background, preparation, and other characteristics. The supervisor must also remember that the same responsibility holds for the student, and, therefore, curiosity on the part of that person about you should not be regarded as prying. The problem of insuring personalized communication is not restricted, however, only to the early days or to the supervisor and trainee as Problem Situation #10 illustrates.

Two-way Street.

Communication can happen only between a minimum of two people. It cannot consist of purpose and personalization on the part of only one person and by that person only. The supervising teacher must always remember his "superior" position in the supervisory arrangement and be aware that the student teacher may be more than a little hesitant to express his true opinions unless prodded. The supervisor must exercise initiative to insure that communication is two-way by encouraging questions designed to discover intent, and by not being sensitive to queries from the student teacher which may at times appear personal.

Listening.

Most student teaching supervisors do too much talking and not enough listening. This is a most serious detriment to positive communication. This, too, is one of the major criticisms voiced by student teachers. "My supervising teacher did all of the talking, and never seemed to listen to what I had to say." Positive communication is characterized by at least equal amounts of listening and talking. All supervisors would do well to check their own personal ratio of each. This topic will be further developed later in this book.

Acceptance.

It is most critical that all parties who communicate be willing to accept the other's positions and points of view. Acceptance does not necessarily imply endorsement of the other's viewpoints, but rather a willingness on the part of the listener to grant at least initial legitimacy to the speaker's position or point. Conversations which begin, "I know you may not agree," certainly provide a clue about the speaker's interpretation of his fellow communicator's frame of reference. Differences in age, experience, and personal philosophy are commonplace between student and supervising teacher. Most college supervisors will testify that communication becomes far more positive between the two after it has become personalized; both parties listening and talking to each other, and both willing to accept the other's *right* to his position. Time has a rather amazing way of reconciling what would appear at first to be irreconcilable differences. An occasional remembrance of Voltaire's statement, "I may disagree with your beliefs, but I defend to the death your right to express them," can do much to insure this process.

Problem Situation #11

Bob, a student teacher who experienced early difficulties but who was willing to accept supervisory help and did make progress, tells his college supervisor that he now hesitates to ask for help from the supervising teacher because the final evaluation time is near.

Openness.

The very nature of the student-supervisor arrangement is threatening to positive communication. Supervisors must remember that students

Supervising teachers need to understand the anxieties of a neophyte.

often try to hide weaknesses from the teacher. But then, many teachers have spent their educational lifetime attempting the same disguise of weakness from department chairmen and principals. A teacher education relationship, on the other hand, if it is to truly result in growth and development, must be predicated upon an openness of expression among all parties concerned. Supervising teachers must not feel threatened by the younger student teacher who may be, because of his newness, more popular with the pupils. The supervising teacher must likewise not feel that communicating to the college supervisor evidences of student teacher inadequacies will be an expression of his own supervisory inadequacy. And certainly, college supervisors should not engage in missions of "search and destroy." The professional supervising teacher can do much to encourage openness on the part of the student teacher by communicating his own personal feelings. It is sincerely hoped, however, that these personalized experiences will be more positive than negative.

Empathy.

Being willing to put yourself in "the other fellow's shoes" is one of the clearest indicators of interest in positive communication. The supervising teacher must always be aware that he is party to a process in which the student is both that and a peer at the same time; a student because of his lack of experience and need to learn; and yet, of necessity, a peer if the instructional process in the classroom is to be most successful. The supervising teacher will need to understand the anxieties of the neophyte, and yet take care not to permit excuses of inexperience, other classes, work, or social activities to be used as an excuse for non-performance. Understanding is what is expected. It will require a delicate balance between a "mother hen" and "der Fuhrer" attitude to accomplish it.[1] It is, once again, the supervising teacher's responsibility to initiate this aspect of positive communication.

Clarity.

One of the truest characteristics of differing generations seems to be their inability to understand clearly what each other means. Not all student and supervising teachers will be of differing generations,

---

[1] The film, *Supervisory Roles with Student Teachers*, available from the Audio-Visual Center of Indiana State University, utilizes role playing to illustrate four exaggerated supervisory roles. It can be used to generate discussion by providing a focus on the various roles that supervising teachers can assume as they work with student teachers.

but even a difference of a few years will probably mean that they speak a different language. This difference may involve both the vernacular and educationese context and not infrequently a differing philosophy. Positive communication, particularly in its earliest stages, should invariably include a great many, "What do you mean by that's?". Once again, it is the supervisor's responsibility to exercise initiative in the request for clarifications. It is the rare student who will initiate such requests of his supervisor. The supervisor can help such a two-way exchange by frequently inquiring whether the student teacher knows what is intended and further by requesting that the student teacher interpret the conversation from his own frame of reference.

Includes Variety.

Positive communication is not always talking or listening. It also includes written responses as well as those non-verbal activities in which we all engage. Non-verbal indicators have received recent attention in both the popular[2] and professional presses.[3] Supervisors must be aware that conferencing trainees in a crowded faculty lounge, locating observers always in the back of the room, failing to introduce students to faculty and support staff, excluding or not informing them of faculty parking and lounges, or using a desk to separate the conference relationships communicates as effectively in non-verbal ways as words either spoken or written.

These characteristics of positive communication are not intended to be all inclusive. Neither are they intended to characterize only that level of communication which attends to the good. Rather, it is hoped that the supervising teacher will regard communication as one of his primary responsibilities, and that he will be aware of the characteristics which differentiate between that which is a good and bad communication level.

[2] Eric Berne, *Games People Play: The Psychology of Human Relationships* (New York: Grove Press, Inc., 1964).

Julius Fast, *Body Language* (New York: M. Evans and Co. Inc., 1970).

Edward D. Hall, *The Silent Language* (Greenwich, Connecticut: Fawcett Publication Inc., 1959).

————, *The Hidden Dimension* (New York: Doubleday Co. Inc., 1966).

Gerald D. Nierenberg and Henry H. Coleho, *How to Read a Person Like a Book* (New York: Pocket Books, Division of Simon and Schuster, Inc., 1973).

[3] Daniel Michalak, *Non Verbal Behavior in Supervisory Conferences* (paper presented, National Clinic on Supervision for the Association of Teacher Educators, Indiana University, Bloomington, Indiana, 1971).

COMMUNICATION DEVICES

Formal.

Devices, such as applications or autobiographical forms, placement requests, contracts or agreements, handbooks or guides, and prepared papers and addresses are usually printed and almost invariably addressed to a generalized audience. They are usually, however, quite specific in purpose and dispassionate in their approach. They are intended to furnish the "facts, and nothing but the facts," and little more. Such communications frequently cause displeasure because they are impersonal and lack opportunity for two-way communication. Usually, however, their purpose is clear and has been carefully prepared to insure clarity. The only way for supervising teachers to overcome the two prime objections is to insist on personalized interpretation from the college supervisor and to communicate their feelings, both positive and negative, to the college administrators responsible.

It has become fairly common to find individual supervising teachers and school systems entering into this formalized communications area. Such devices as school-derived application forms and agreements and building or teacher-prepared handbooks or guides are certainly not uncommon and are to be highly recommended because they clarify positions. It is sincerely hoped that the entry of supervising teachers and administrators into the arena of prepared papers and addresses will likewise be forthcoming. In fact, a book in supervision written by a practicing supervising teacher is long over-due. Public school personnel have a great communications contribution to make and until such time as they accept the responsibility for writing and speaking, the formal street will remain largely "One-Way."

Informal.

Most daily communications are of this variety. They include written, spoken, and non-verbal efforts in planned and casual conversations, conferences, notes, letters, telephone calls, appearances, and actions. Most are not planned beyond a general outline or intent and many are spur-of-the-moment at best. They are when we are most apt to reveal the real us because we have taken few pains to plan or hide our intent. The real problem is that they are when we exercise the least care to communicate adequately, and yet when we communicate the most.

Certainly none of the foregoing should be interpreted by any supervising teacher as meaning that informal communications with the student trainee are to be avoided or even limited. Rather, the supervisor needs to be aware that students attach far more meaning and read interpretations far beyond intent into the grumpy "Good morning" or the "See you tomorrow" when tomorrow is Saturday, than we frequently recognize. One of the clearest indications to the experienced college supervisor of the student-supervising teacher relationship is the degree to which informal communication takes place. Problems almost assuredly exist when conversations between the two concern only the absolute necessities of instruction and relationship; when conferences are held only on a strictly scheduled basis; when notes are almost always threatening, when telephone calls are apt to be reminders, and invariably when such informal contacts are mostly supervising teacher initiated.

Here again, the supervising teacher is primarily responsible for establishing the nature and degree of informal communications. Even before the arrival of the student teacher, why not telephone or write a friendly note inviting early contact and expressing interest and enthusiasm? Attention to housing accommodations and classroom provisions including texts and materials, a peer seating and desk arrangement, a mailbox and inclusion on the faculty distribution list, and certainly introductions to the faculty *and* staff of the building will do far more to set the tone of relationship than all of the formalized, engraved notices that have ever been printed.

Supervising teachers sometimes worry about whether communicating too informally may not interfere with or even prevent their making a supervisory input. Some of them remember the admonition of their general methods instructor who emphatically stated, "Start tough and you can always loosen up." It would be well to remember that the statement was intended to describe classroom management and also those between a teacher and pupils. Supervision of a student teacher or other types of trainees rarely finds itself at the discipline stage. Further, it is predicated upon a peer relationship. The only real care that supervising teachers need exercise is that their trainees are always able to distinguish between the informal when it is intended to be casual and when it means business.

Problem Situation #12

A very angry letter from a supervising teacher addressed to the Director of Student Teaching demands an explanation of why the Handbook for Student Teaching insists on the importance of daily written lesson plans and then why the college supervisor on his visit casually remarked that he did not have time to look at them.

Verbal.

Just a sentence or two here to remind the reader that verbal communications can be written or spoken, formal or informal in nature. All of us tend to be more careful in our written, formal types of communications and frequently more than a little careless in our spoken, informal kinds. Likewise, most of us tend to use the former for negative criticisms and the latter for praise. It might be well occasionally to check both varieties to insure a balance.

Non-Verbal.

This type of communication has received a goodly amount of publicity recently because of the advent of the "T-Group" and similar movements as well as the publication of popular books[4] which stress the importance of non-verbal communication. The authors are not advocates of the "feel and touch and gaze deeply sensitivity movement," although aspects of awareness are critical to communication. Neither do they go to the lengths of some authors in attaching to every posture, movement, or gesture a symbolic meaning. Obviously what is done does have interpretable meaning for others. To imply, however, that physical actions always have the same meaning or are done for the same reason would appear more than a little mechanistic and over-simplified. Supervisors can help trainees see their actions through the eyes of another and from the perspective of the pupils. Not infrequently what has become an acceptable campus behavior pattern (sitting cross-legged on the edge of a desk in a micro-mini) may not be recognized by the student teacher as having a different interpretation in a public school setting. The supervising teacher, too, will exemplify certain non-verbal characteristics. Recognizing that the student teacher has become a "mirror-image" of yourself can be disconcerting, and particularly so, if you ask yourself, "why?".

Supervisors communicate in a great many ways with student trainees. A variety of techniques and devices should be employed. Supervisors should be conscious of the purposes and limitations of them and give some thought to the degree to which the relative types are used.

COMMUNICATION FUNDAMENTALS

The following do not fit the description of either characteristics or devices but are important considerations if one is concerned about improvement of the communication process.

[4]Thomas A. Harris, *I'm OK—You're OK* (New York and Evanston: Harper & Row, 1967).

Constantly Occurs.

Communication is one of those rare things that just happens. It does not depend upon intent or even action. Not talking, not reading, not listening, or not responding carries a message and sometimes speaks louder than the reverse of the actions. The message here for supervisors is that since you will communicate whether you like it or not, you might as well make the best of it and communicate what you intend.

Purpose Is Paramount.

Communication without purpose will result in confusion, misunderstanding, and unhappy team members. The first section of this chapter presented the positive results achieved when communication is characterized as being purposeful. The intent here is to emphasize once again that when the negative conditions are found, it is time to examine the communications process for possible lack of clearly defined and understood purposes.

Communication Vs. Conferences.

A most common response by the supervising teacher to an inquiry of a college supervisor regarding some problem involving the student teacher is, "We haven't had time to have a conference about that yet." The implication is that either the problem is so enormous that it requires a formal conference, or that the supervising teacher regards the conference as the only time and place for communication. Problems which must wait for conferences frequently tend to become magnified out of proportion and give a negative orientation. Communications and conferences operate at their highest level when they assume the characteristic of continuous dialogue.

Personality Conflicts.

Personality is obviously a factor which conditions the supervisory relationship. It may not, however, be permitted as an excuse for not communicating by either the student or supervising teacher or the college supervisor. In that extremely rare situation where parties are hopelessly matched, the solution can only be a change of assignment rather than a decision not to communicate. Growth and development is so totally dependent upon positive communication that the latter decision must be regarded as unacceptable.

SUMMARY

Communication, by its very nature, is the essence of instruction; communication not only between teacher and pupils, but also that process by which supervisor and trainee interact. The act itself means "to impart" and "to acquire." This is the purpose of supervision and teacher training. Communication can be either positive or negative; that is, either accomplish its intended goals or impede them. Obviously, only the former is considered commendable.

This chapter has tried to describe communication in terms of those factors which help to make it positive and to describe the various kinds of communication devices. Throughout these two sections and the final one on Fundamentals, the theme has been that though all parties to the training process have a responsibility for insuring positive communication, it is the supervising teacher who by virtue of his position must bear the heaviest responsibility. Communication is always taking place; good communication may happen in spite of what we do; but the best, most positive communication requires purpose, planning, and thoughtful execution.

CHAPTER FIVE

Planning Techniques

Principals:	How can I identify the best potential supervising teachers from within my staff?
	How can I convince parents that teacher education students are not a handicap to their children's education?
Directors of Student Teaching:	How can I help develop a more meaningful relationship between campus courses and the field experiences?
	How can I help develop an effective partnership between the schools and the college?
Student Teachers:	How can I make the best possible initial impression on my supervising teacher and college supervisor?
	How can I get the kids to like me and still work for me?
Supervising Teachers:	How can I help my pupils to accept my student teacher as a teacher?
	How can the college supervisor and I work most effectively together to help the student teacher?
College Supervisors:	How can I best communicate the college's expectations to the student and supervising teacher?
	How can I make my maximum contribution to the "team's" supervisory effort?

The establishment of effective positive communication is absolutely essential in any quality supervisory relationship as was described in the previous chapter. That communication must have purpose was a primary premise. This chapter and its focus on planning may be regarded as the medium employed to insure that purpose is planned. The instances of planning as presented in the above Problem Situation are used to illustrate that a variety of people must plan in a variety of ways in any situation involving students in teacher education. All too frequently supervision texts, college supervisors, student teachers, and supervising teachers are of the opinion that planning is appropriate only in terms of formalized lesson plans prepared in connection with classroom instruction. This seems to place the full burden for planning upon the shoulders of the student teacher. Such is not the intent of this chapter. A most basic premise is that all parties to the teacher education process must be involved with planning. The greatest hope for success can only lie in each individual's realization of his responsibilities and will be best demonstrated by his actions. None of this can occur without an awareness of planning techniques as they affect each individual's role. The basic purpose of this chapter, then, is to provide suggested planning techniques as they most directly relate to the interaction between supervising and student teachers and the others most directly involved in the teacher education process.

The true importance of planning lies in the acceptance of it as an absolute necessity as opposed to the niceties of any particular style, format, or length. In other words, it is far more important that supervising teachers and student teachers regard planning as absolutely necessary than that they become embroiled, perhaps even with the college supervisor, in lengthy discussions of the nature and style of lesson plans themselves. This chapter, then, will concern itself not so much with the specific details of planning *per se,* but rather with trying to provide the general framework within which individual latitude may be exercised so that planning can accomplish its only real end; that is, improvement of the learning process.

CHARACTERISTICS OF GOOD PLANNING

Purposeful.

If the true purpose is the resultant improvement of instruction or other activities, then it seems logical that it can best accomplish this purpose if it is intentionally done. "Accidental" or "incidental" learning certainly exists. We have all learned many things without having planned to do so. Any educational program, however, which used either of these two techniques as its process would be grossly inefficient. The degree to which planning is purposeful and has as its purpose the improvement of instruction is one of the true distinguishing characteristics of the professional teacher-educator.

Pre-planned.

Another important characteristic of planning is that is happens sufficiently far in advance so that it can be previewed and analyzed by the supervising teacher and modified if necessary by the student teacher prior to the time that the actual instruction takes place. All too frequently conferences which follow instruction on the part of the student teacher tend to be negative because the supervising teacher is reacting to something he would not have approved if he had known about it in advance. It would, thus, seem obvious that if planning is to best serve the purpose of learning and development on the part of the student teacher that it only can be accomplished if pre-plans are available for the supervising teacher's reaction prior to the time that they are used. This pre-planning need in no way interfere with the initiative of the student teacher or be so structured as to limit flexibility at the time the instruction is implemented. The purpose of pre-planning is to provide opportunity for the supervising teacher to insure that only the best instruction takes place. It might also be pointed out that being aware in advance of what is planned is the supervising teacher's best legal safeguard in any instance where the liability of the student teacher and supervising teacher might be questioned because of negligence on the part of either. No formula exists to provide guidance for the length of time that plans should be submitted by pre-analysis by the supervising teacher. The length of time must obviously be conditioned by the local situation, but in all instances must allow sufficient time for modification of the plan if need so dictates.

Insures Instructional or Operational Security.

All planning which involves instruction on the part of the student teacher, or which involves activities which are operational in nature as opposed to instructional, must involve planning which insures the safety and security of the learners. This is a prime responsibility of the supervising teacher, since he by virtue of his certification and experience is the only one in the classroom charged with that legal responsibility. No plan should be approved which does not give the best assurance of guaranteeing instructional and operational security on the part of the learner. And no instruction or supervision should be permitted for which prior planning has not been done. Learning on the part of the school's pupils must always be the prime consideration as opposed to the desirability of instructional intent on the part of the student teacher.

Risk Oriented.

All planning which is to result in growth on the part of the student teacher will usually have a certain risk element involved. This statement does not imply that the risk be at the expense of the pupils, but rather that the supervising teacher must be willing to allow trial of techniques and/or methods which on the surface may not appear workable, at least within the ability or opinion of the supervising teacher. To the extent that the student teacher may try only those things that have worked successfully for the supervising teacher, *he can become no more than a copy*. It would seem far better for the student teacher to try risk-oriented activities at the time he has the security which experienced supervising teachers can provide than to wait until he is a first year teacher in his own room and without the help of the experienced teacher to assist. Risk-oriented should never, however, be the justification for unplanned instruction on the part of either a student teacher or any other type of participant. Risk, rather, implies opportunity to try pre-planned activities that are not ordinarily used by the supervisor—not advance endorsement of "doing your own thing."

Problem Situation #14

> A very frustrated and discouraged student has called his college supervisor to request permission to withdraw from student teaching because as he says, "No matter how I try or how hard I work I just can't teach like my supervising teacher. I can't achieve the same results with the pupils using her techniques. I just will never be as good a teacher as she is. She encourages me to try teaching in my own way, but it is so poor by comparison with what she does that even I know it's bad."

Provides for Alternative Opportunity.

Planning at its best provides for individualization of instruction or activity, flexibility in the way such instruction is accomplished, and evidence of creativity on the part of both the learner and the teacher. It is most difficult for these goals to be accomplished if the supervising teacher insists on rigid adherence to his particular style and format. Just as the supervising teacher recognizes that not all pupils learn in the same way, so must he recognize that rarely can his student teacher best accomplish instruction if he is required to be a carbon copy of the supervising teacher. Insuring that the student teacher develop his own personalized teaching style will require that the supervising teacher at times be prepared to "cut the cord" and yet in other instances be prepared to "haul back on the reins." Much of the supervising teacher's success in this area will depend upon his awareness of the student teacher's competence and confidence at the varying stages of student teaching.

Student Teacher Initiated.

The phrase, "Mother, I would rather do it myself!", characterizes this intent. Most of us would prefer to bear responsibility for personally planning those activities for which we are responsible. It should not come as a surprise to any supervising teacher to find that the student teacher feels the same. This is not to imply that the student teacher should be given complete responsibility for the determination of all planning throughout the student teaching period. Obviously in the earliest days and weeks, most student teachers will need to depend rather heavily upon planning developed by the supervising teacher and/or as found in curriculum guides and similar sources. It is the supervising teacher's responsibility, however, to insure that the student teacher, even though possibly unwilling, gradually develops his own plans so that by the end of the period of student teaching he is a self-initiated planner. Even at this stage, however, the supervising teacher still must bear responsibility for review and analysis of the student teacher's plans.

Basis for Analysis and Evaluation of Growth and Performance.

A final characteristic of all types of planning must be that it furnishes a true basis for analysis and evaluation. Pre-developed plans are the measurement yardstick against which both the student and supervising teacher can make some judgment with respect to how well the instructional intent has been accomplished. This evaluation is intended to be an indicator not only of the present level of performance, but can also furnish a continuing indicator of growth on the part of the student teacher. It is important that the supervising teacher view plans developed by the student teacher not only as something to be previewed and analyzed and modified in advance and used to provide the structure for instruction; but then also as the medium for analysis and evaluation of what was intended.

These characteristics of planning have run the full cycle of any good instructional process beginning with purpose and ending with evaluation. The basic intent is that the involvement of the student and supervising teacher exemplify exactly the same instructional characteristics as the student teacher is expected to represent in the classrooms that he teaches.

RESPONSIBILITIES OF THE TEAM MEMBERS INVOLVED

Although the preparation of actual plan is regarded as the primary responsibility of the teacher trainee, it must be viewed as a team effort action with each of the members aware of and accepting his responsibility. These responsibilities cover a wide range of activities and include such responsibilities as serving as an exemplar of well-planned instruction, furnishing basic planning instruction, encouraging and if necessary insisting on planning being done, critiquing of student prepared plans, recommending modifications, utilizing the plans as a basis for objectifying observations, and helping the student to evaluate his instructional efforts within the context of the pre-prepared plans. One of the major impediments which has traditionally prevented planning from producing better teachers has been the lack of concerted effort and accepted responsibility on the part of the various involved parties. All too frequently the student teacher has been held singularly responsible for his planning inadequacies. The purpose of Figure 5:1 is to identify the individuals who must assume an active role if planning is to achieve its maximum effectiveness.

Figure 5:1 Composition of the Planning Team

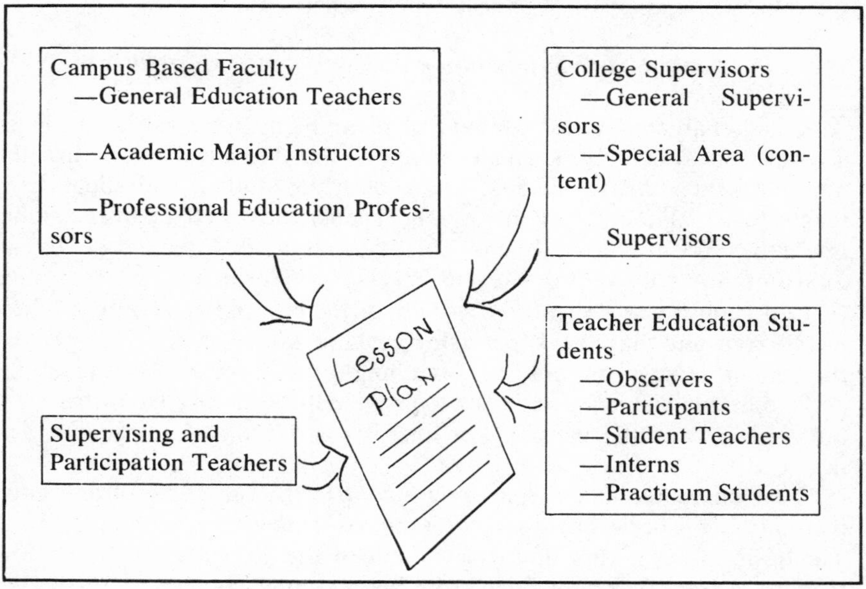

Campus Based Faculty
—General Education Teachers

—Academic Major Instructors

—Professional Education Professors

Supervising and Participation Teachers

College Supervisors
—General Supervisors
—Special Area (content)

Supervisors

Teacher Education Students
—Observers
—Participants
—Student Teachers
—Interns
—Practicum Students

Lesson Plan

Campus Based Faculty.

The campus faculty bears responsibility for the initial preparation of the teacher education student in the field of planning. This responsibility varies with respect to the type of college faculty member involved. For example, faculty members who are responsible for the general education and content or major preparation areas have a responsibility not only to provide the teacher education student with the basic foundations necessary for his functioning as a prospective teacher; but also to exemplify by their instructional behavior, knowledge of the principles of planning and their acceptance of planning as an important characteristic. This is most critical in terms of those professors who are responsible for the instruction of students in their major areas. Obviously student teachers, just as all of us are inclined to do, will teach as they were taught. To the extent that they are taught with little evidence of adequate prior planning and preparation, so will they tend to exhibit the same behavior.

It is not unusual to find the general education and content faculty unacquainted with sound principles of planning, but it is inexcusable for those education faculty who are responsible for the professional education preparation of prospective teachers not to be aware of and exemplify in every respect adequate concepts of planning. This is particularly true with respect to methods instructors. These instructors bear prime responsibility for acquainting the prospective teacher with the principles of planning. These must include not only an awareness of the necessary components of adequate planning but also an understanding of the psychological and physiological attributes of pupils at the appropriate level which will most influence learning. These methods instructors have responsibility for familiarizing the teacher trainee with the various levels of planning; that is, ranging from the most global approach such as resource units and teaching units to the most minute level, the daily lesson plan. They are also responsible for developing in the student an awareness of the four basic parts of a lesson plan; that is, objectives, activities, materials, and evaluation. They can make a great contribution by helping the student clarify the purpose and nature of objectives and the variety of activities and resource materials that are available to implement the instructional process. They must also require the teacher trainee to prepare a variety of plans, to analyze and evaluate these plans, and to assist the trainee in the modification of those plans to most effectively implement instruction. Methods instructors must take great care not to overstructure planning to the extent that only a single model or format is deemed acceptable by the teacher trainee. If such is done, it will invariably create a situation of conflict for the teacher trainee and the supervising teacher who may not be familiar with the exacting expectations of the college or university methods instructor.

In summary, then, the campus faculty is expected to exemplify by its attitude and its behavior a belief in planning and even more importantly to practice what it believes. The professional education faculty has additional responsibility for the initial training of the teacher education student in the intricacies of planning. This faculty must also provide experience for the student in the development of actual plans and assist the student in the analysis and refinement of those plans. All of this must happen before the trainee is ready to go into the field as an effective beginning instructor.

Supervising Teacher.

Whereas the campus faculty was charged with the responsibility for the basic instruction of the teacher trainee in planning techniques, the supervising teacher bears the even heavier responsibility for implementation of adequate planning techniques at the "use" level. The teacher's responsibility is classified as "heavier" simply because all types of planning done by the student teacher will directly involve learning by the pupils of the school. The planning done on the university campus was usually assigned only as an exercise in learning and was, rarely if ever, strictly applicable to pupil learning.

A supervising teacher has a vast number of responsibilities. These include: (1) believing in the importance of planning, (2) exemplifying by his behavior the practice of this belief, (3) acquainting himself with the planning techniques taught by the campus faculty and desired for use by the student teacher during the student teaching period, (4) acquainting the student teacher with the courses and/or subjects being taught—their general composition, specific units, progress of the pupils to the point of entry of the student teacher, and expectations of the local school and community, (5) familiarizing the student teacher with the variety and extent of instructional activities and material resources available, (6) familiarizing the student teacher with the physical and learning characteristics of the pupils, (7) being willing to devote the inordinate amount of time necessary to work with the student teacher on the preview, analysis, modification, and evaluation of the plans as they directly affect instruction, and (8) being willing to insist, if all else fails, on the absolute necessity for plans prior to the student teacher's assumption of instructional responsibility.

The above listing, though extensive, is not intended to be exhaustive. It certainly does indicate, however, the supervising teacher's responsibility. Not all of the items are of equal weight; several are obviously far more critical than others. The two most critical are that the supervising teacher be familiar with techniques of planning and the expectations of the college or university, and secondly that the supervising teacher be willing to insist on the absolute requirement that no instruction on the part of the student teacher be permitted without prior planning having been done.

All good teachers plan. It is assumed that supervising teachers are no exception to this statement. It will undoubtedly be true that supervising teachers, just as any experienced teachers, perform planning at different levels and in different styles than will the neophyte student teacher. It is also true that the supervising teacher's knowledge of planning techniques may not coincide with that being taught on campus. As a consequence, the supervising teacher's definitions may be at some variance with the expectations that the student teacher has from the college or university. Most colleges or universities in their student teaching handbooks and other similar types of materials attempt to clarify the planning style and suggested planning techniques to help the supervising teacher gain a clearer idea of what is expected of the student. The college supervisor should also be able to help in this clarification of expectations. The supervising teacher should not hesitate to contact on-campus faculty members, particularly the methods instructors, with the request that he be furnished the kinds of learning materials with respect to planning that were furnished to the student teacher. The student teacher might also be asked to allow the supervising teacher to look at lesson plans and unit plans that he had prepared to fulfill the campus expectation. The chapter on communications techniques listed many items that could or should be communicated between the various parties involved in teacher education. Certainly one of the most critical and important of the items that needs to be communicated is planning techniques. The chapter on observation techniques will make it clear that the primary thrust of observation must be a concern with observing how well planning is implemented. The chapter on conferencing techniques also recommends that many conferences between the supervising teacher and student teacher and also between those two and the college supervisor center around planning, its techniques, execution, and evaluation. These latter illustrations are cited simply to reinforce the premise that planning is so absolutely fundamental and important that without attention to it there is little hope for growth and development on the part of the student teacher.

Throughout all of the process the supervising teacher must bear the prime responsibility for not only seeing that planning is done, but also for doing whatever is necessary to insure that the student teacher through his planning exhibits growth. This cannot be done if the student teacher is expected or required to strictly model or emulate the supervising teacher's pattern and/or plans. The student teacher should be expected and even required if necessary to exhibit individuality in the preparation of plans. At the same time the supervising teacher has every right to expect that the student teacher has an adequate rationale for such innovation. One of the best ways to insure that student teachers have reasons for what they are doing is to ask the question, "Why," rather than the more typical question, "How." This patterning of planning behavior is consistent with a very fundamental premise of this book; that is, the importance of helping the student teacher become a self-developing, self-analytical teacher. Supervising teachers must always keep in mind that their ultimate intent is to produce a student teacher who in his first year will be able to grow and develop beyond where he finished student teaching.

One of the most difficult recognitions for most student teachers is that planning will be a continuing part of their instructional life as long as they are teachers. Many tend to regard it as only a course responsibility during a student teaching period, much as doing a term paper is a course requirement frequently unrelated to real life. The supervising teacher, then, bears an additional responsibility for trying to communicate by his own life style that planning is a continuing component of his teaching life. Perhaps in a different style and certainly a different degree than that experienced during the student teaching period; but a most necessary part nevertheless.

College Supervisor.

The college supervisor at most institutions occupies a unique position in terms of his responsibilities for planning. Frequently the college supervisor has not been the person directly responsible for the methods instruction and as a consequence may not be personally familiar with what has been taught by way of techniques. Even in those situations where he has had an on-campus responsibility for such methods instruction, he would have been responsible for and most familiar with only a single content area. The usual college supervisor will also work with a number of supervising teachers who will undoubtedly represent a variety of training and experience backgrounds. It should also not be overlooked that the college supervisor will be responsible for working with a number of student teachers each of whom will bring his individual learning capacities and abilities to the process. To help counter these problems, some colleges now have their supervisor teach an on-site methods course which is taken by the student teachers during their field experience. The course is often made available to the supervising teachers also. An institution's ability to offer such a course must depend, however, upon the concentration of a number of student teachers within a given building or site. Advantages such as this availability and usefulness of on-site, during-experience courses are undoubtedly the explanation for the rapidly growing number of "center" or "site" type placement arrangements. The college supervisor then is responsible for furnishing the primary communication between the training and expectations of the campus and the training and needs of the supervising teacher's classroom. He thus serves as a translator of both what has been done and a mediator of those expectations into the immediacies of the instructional scene. This means that the college supervisor must take great pains to acquaint himself with the variety of planning techniques taught on the campus, and in addition familiarize himself with the public schools and their supervising teacher. In addition to fulfilling a communicating and translating role, the college supervisor must also serve as a verifier of the performance of the student teacher in connection with planning. This verification role can be subject to misinterpretation by supervising and student teachers. It could be interpreted that the college supervisor in this connection is fulfilling some type of "supersnoop" role. This interpretation, however, would fail to recognize his direct responsibility to verify that the student teacher is fulfilling the expectations of the institution.

Problem Situation #15

A very angry principal has just finished a telephone call to the director of student teaching. He reported that the college supervisor's critical comments about the student teachers' lesson plans have upset his teachers, particularly since at least several of the students were using their supervising teacher's plans. He regards the college supervisor's comments as a reflection on his staff's competence, an interference with the harmony of his building, a reflection on the student's methods instructors, and a lack of sensitivity on the part of the college supervisor. He demands the presence of the director in his school within twenty-four hours.

The most important responsibility of the college supervisor, however, is to serve as a resource for both the supervising and student teacher. This responsibility should include: examination of the student teacher's lesson plans, reinforcement that what is being done is satisfactory, and suggestions for improvement. He should be able to suggest alternative activities and resource materials since he has visited many schools and many classrooms and worked with a variety of methods instructors. He should also reinforce the supervising teacher who may be frustrated by a reluctant planner. The college supervisor's role, however, is not

Planning is an important aspect of student teaching.

to serve as a dictator of planning expectancies and execution, but rather to serve as a team resource member who can help insure that planning takes place at its most effective level.

Student Teacher.

The word, heavy, has been used to describe the responsibility of the three aforementioned types of peoples. It should be obvious though that the superlative, heaviest, must be used to describe the student teacher's responsibility for involvement in the planning process. As was previously mentioned, the student teacher must be the initiator of the plans. Initiation in the earliest stages of student teaching will undoubtedly involve heavy dependence upon the plans of the supervising teacher, and perhaps even those of the campus methods instructors. During the student teaching period, however, the student teacher must gradually and then fully evolve into an independent initiator of his own instructional destiny. This means that the student teacher must be aware of the techniques of planning, accept responsibility for planning, and do it. Unless the student teacher fulfills all three responsibilities, knowing, accepting, and doing; the planning process is incomplete and instructional failure is guaranteed. It is not unusual for college supervisors to hear the lament from the student teacher that his originality, creativity, and freedom are being restricted by the supervising teacher. Such is rarely true if the student teacher in his prior plans has demonstrated to the supervising teacher that he is truly creative and original, and that what is being proposed will insure instructional or operational security. Student teachers must realize that before instructional or operational latitude can be permitted, formalized planning must demonstrate to the satisfaction of his supervising superiors that what is proposed stands at least a chance of successful implementation.

An additional responsibility of the student teacher is to insure that plans are developed and given to the supervising teacher sufficiently in advance of the intended instruction so that reactions by the supervising teacher and modifications, if necessary, can be successfully accomplished prior to use. Student teachers also have a responsibility for not so personally identifying with their creations that they cannot tolerate criticism and/or required modifications. They must understand that the supervising teacher is the only one of the team legally and directly responsible for the instructional and operational activities of the classroom to which he has been assigned. As a consequence the supervising teacher would be negligent in his duties, both to the pupils in his classroom *and* to the student teacher if he did not indicate opportunities for planning improvement.

Observers/Participants.

The increased number and frequency of appearance of pre-student teaching observers and participants in the supervising teacher's classroom is one of the more recent characteristics of teacher education programs. The presence of these new kinds of teacher trainees certainly has implications for planning on the part of both the supervising and student teacher. College supervisors frequently hear the query from supervising teachers, "What should I be doing differently with these people than I do with the student teacher?". Student teachers frequently, too, are at a loss to know what their relationship to and responsibilities are for these observers or participants who may on occasion find themselves within the student teacher's classroom. The prime responsibility for the planning of observer and participant activities must lie with that campus faculty member who is responsible for their being in the school. He must not only be responsible for the planning of the logistics that gets them to the school, but also must be responsible for the planning of the reasons for their being there, and the activities in which he wishes them to engage. Further, he must have planned ways of communicating these expectations to the supervising teachers in the schools, and planned so as to insure that supervision of them happens both from the college or university and the school concerned. The authors strongly believe that building administrators and supervising teachers must accept responsibility for refusing to permit observers and participants in their buildings and/or classrooms for whom such prior planning and communication has not taken place. The observers and participants themselves must take responsibility for knowing what it is that they are expected to do. No irresponsibility on the part of the campus faculty with respect to observers and/or participants or lack of responsibility on the part of the building administrators or supervising teachers is intended by the previous statement. Rather, the increased emphasis upon this level of pre-student teaching experiences is so new that much still remains to be planned to insure a meaningful scope and sequence for these learning activities. In fact, the traditional one student teacher to one supervising teacher relationship has many disadvantages. Team teaching in the public schools has certainly demonstrated the efficiency of multiple instructional personnel within the confines of a single room. Such success has possible implications for the meaningful placement of multiple teacher education trainees with a single supervising teacher or team of teachers. Much, however, still needs to be done in terms of determining optimal numbers of such trainees and the role and responsibility relationships of each to the others.

ESSENTIAL COMPONENTS OF PLANS

The very nature of planning implies some type of organization or structure. This attention to organization or structure must also be a part of the planning process itself. A wide variety of formats for lesson plans exists, as was previously mentioned. The authors each have their individual favorite forms, but collectively are in agreement that no plan can be considered complete which does not contain at least four fundamental sections: objectives, activities, materials, and evaluation. In addition, the format needs to identify the who, what, where, and when characteristics of the instruction and may also be divided into teacher and pupil sections. The sample lesson plan format as presented in Figure 5.2 is provided only for diagramatic illustration of these points. It is not presented as either a perfect type or to limit modification by any party in the planning team.

Objectives.

Every instructional act, if it is to maximize the potential for learning, must begin with a statement of what is to be accomplished. This is not intended to avoid the implication of accidental or incidental learning, but reliance on such free-wheeling design is one of the surest characteristics of the practitioner as opposed to the professional teacher-educator.

Figure 5:2 Sample Lesson Plan Format

Preparer's Name: _____ School:_____

Subject/Grade Level: _____ Topic/Unit:_____

Date Use Intended: _____ Time Span Intended:_____

Relationship to Prior & Future Instruction	I. *Objectives* (pupils)	(teacher)
Time Allotment	II. *Activities* (pupils)	(teacher)
Source	III. *Materials Needed* (pupils)	(teacher)
	IV. *Evaluation* (pupils)	(teacher)

Assignment: (growing out of this plan)
Motivation: (intended to insure assignment completion)

A discussion of objectives which begins with a semantic debate of whether this first component is most appropriately labeled objectives, purposes, aims or competencies is not considered either important or critical. It is imperative, however, that the student and supervising teacher recognize that whatever they are called that they be present. Figure 5:3 schematically illustrates this point.

Supervising teachers need to exercise great care to prevent the student teacher from viewing this first component as simply a content outline of the material to be taught. It must include a complete description of what is to be accomplished presented in terms of categorized items as opposed to a chronological presentation of the instructional totality. This first section of a plan includes an analysis of content in terms of the facts to be learned, the skills to be mastered, the concepts to be understood, and the attitudes, and appreciation to be developed. Not every lesson will or should include all four levels. But certainly the student teacher must have made prior analysis of what constitutes the learning in terms of these categories. The method of presentation

Figure 5:3 Structure of Objectives

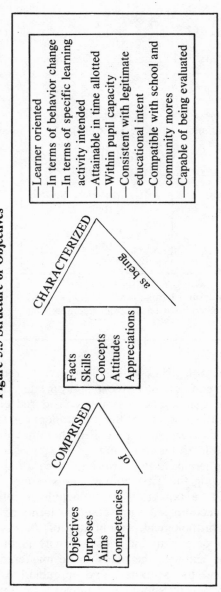

of facts, skills, concepts, attitudes, and appreciation may range from the most general to the highly specific. For example, at the most general level, facts might include "to memorize the causes of the Revolutionary War." At the most specific level, these would include a detailed listing of all of the causes. The degree to which the student teacher is required in his planning to be general or specific has relationship to the phase of student teaching. In the initial phases, it would seem wise to require plans at a quite specific level. In later phases when the student teacher has acquired confidence and has exhibited competence, it may be possible to permit a more generalized presentation of objectives, but still expressed in terms of the four subdivisions. Some care must be exercised, however, that the generalized statement of objectives is not so general as not to lend itself to evaluation. For example, a general objective in a social studies-government class might be "to learn to be a participating member of a democratic society." If the intent of the instructional activity is to teach the students how to operate a voting machine, it would seem far better to so describe that activity in the objectives than to express it in such a generalized fashion that evaluation is virtually impossible. All objectives, it will be noted, should be expressed in terms of the learner; that is, "to learn" rather than "to teach." So expressing objectives may appear to be a rather petty and inconsequential item, but the intent is to force the student teacher to recognize that his instructional success can only be measured in terms of the degree to which his pupils have learned as opposed to whether he has successfully taught.

It should be clearly understood by the supervising teacher that throughout all of this process that the student teacher is in truth a learner also. He is a learner who needs objectives for his teaching, activities, materials, and an evaluation of how successful he was as a teacher. Some quite successful supervising teachers have devised a technique for dividing the objectives section of the plan into pupil objectives and student teacher objectives. Thus it is possible in the post-observation conference to consider both the success of the instructional activity as it relates to pupil learning and to the success of the teacher. Requiring the student teacher to characterize the facts, skills, concepts, or attitudes and appreciation in terms of the learning activity expected will do much to insure that the activities selected will be consistent with the expectations.

The expression of intended pupil activity can range from the most general "to learn" to the quite specific "to read," "to recall," "to memorize," "to be able to list . . .," "to be able to reorder four items in their chronological order," "to be able to hop six times on one foot in ten seconds," etc. Although it is possible to express activity in terms

of such general statements as "to learn," "to understand," "to compre-
hend," or "to appreciate,"; it is virtually impossible to evaluate such
generalities, and as a consequence student teachers should always describe
as specifically as possible the nature of the activity expected.

Of the four essential components of any plan, objectives are the most
important and most fundamental. Objectives are what determine activities
on the part of both the teacher and the pupils. Objectives will determine
the instructional materials to be used, and finally evaluation will of
absolute necessity be mandated by the intent of the instruction. The
objectives section of a plan is not only the most important, but will
as a consequence require the most immediate and careful attention of
the supervising teacher. The supervising teacher must devote major
attention to this section of the plan and through such attention demonstrate
that he is truly a professional. The professional teacher is far more
concerned with the structuring of learning than with the activities or
materials used to accomplish it. The professional recognizes that the
definition of what is to be learned is critical. The supervising teacher
is that professional at the local level who is most aware of the appropriateness of what is proposed for instructional activity, the best qualified
professional to make decisions in terms of whether the instruction
proposed is attainable in the time periods allotted, and whether it is
acceptable in terms of the local school's curriculum, patterns, and mores.
It is not unusual for student teachers to be unaware of local curricular
expectations. As a consequence, the supervising teacher needs to be
conscious of the student's limitations in this respect and take steps
to insure that he fulfills his responsibilities.

Supervising teachers bear the prime responsibility for insuring that
adequate attention is placed upon determination of the objectives for
instruction or operation. They may find several of the publications listed
in the bibliography which deal with the structuring of objectives useful.
Consultation with the college supervisor and the campus methods teachers
may also prove of value in insuring that planning truly pays attention
to this most important component.

Activities.

The component, activities, is a logical outgrowth of those things that
must be done to insure accomplishment of the instructional intent as
described in the first section, objectives. Listing of activities is typically
arranged in a chronological order beginning with the first activity of
the instructional period and concluding with the end of the time period.
It may be well, particularly in the initial stages of the student teaching
period, to require the student teacher to make some time estimation

for each activity. This forces the student teacher to make some estimation and analysis, not only of the anticipated length of time needed, but also of the relative time value of each activity. For example, if the student teacher indicates that more time will be allowed for the taking of attendance than for the concluding summary and evaluation activities, the supervising teacher may well wish to raise a question about appropriate allocation of time.

It is possible within this section to divide the activities intended into two or even three sections. One of these consists of pupil-oriented activities; that is what the pupils are to do at each stage of the time period. The second section which may be considered optional, though it is strongly suggested in the early stages, is entitled teacher activities. This will help insure that the student teacher recognize that for each pupil activity there is a consequent teacher activity. This technique will emphasize for those student teachers who are self-centered that most of their activity is teacher-centered as opposed to pupil-centered. The third categorization of activity may be regarded as purely optional. Once again, however, it is strongly suggested. This section would be entitled, "supervising teacher activity." It serves the dual purpose of fully clarifying for both the student and supervising teacher the nature of what the supervising teacher will be doing as well as emphasizing the "team" arrangement of the experience.

Problem Situation #16

Karen relates to the college supervisor both tearfully and heatedly that her supervising teacher frequently interjects himself into the classroom activities without any prior indication that he was expected to participate. She feels that such action is threatening to her pupils accepting her as their teacher.

A most frequent student teacher criticism is that he is unaware of and unprepared for the activities of the supervising teacher during the time that *he is* responsible for instruction. Making the supervising teacher activities a part of the pre-planning will help insure that both the student and supervising teacher are aware of each other's intended activities and responsibilities. This might help avoid what is described in Problem Situation #16.

The supervising teacher's responsibilities with respect to planning by the student teacher for the activities component would include: (1) insuring that the description of activity is commensurate with the objectives as stated within the first section. Quite frequently student teachers will list objectives for which it seems no instructional activity is provided. Conversely it is not uncommon for instructional activity to be described for which no apparent instructional objective has been listed, (2) insuring that the activities are appropriate to the instructional objective. This would include attention to the appropriateness of the activity for the age and learning level of the pupils and the content to be taught, (3) insuring that the activities listed provide the greatest promise of instructional efficiency. Student teachers occasionally seem unaware that doing things in different ways produces different results. The supervising teacher must exercise some caution at this point, however, that he does not judge the activity and its anticipated efficiency in terms of his own instructional abilities. He must recognize that he and the student teacher represent, at least potentially, two different capacities and as such the student teacher may of necessity require the opportunity to utilize activities best suited to his teaching style and personality, (4) insuring that the instructional activities represent a variety of techniques. The student teacher will undoubtedly find it most comfortable to begin by patterning his activities on those practiced by the supervising teacher. There is nothing wrong with this. In fact, it may be highly desirable since the pupils are accustomed to a certain pattern of activities and procedures. As the student teaching period progresses, however, the supervising teacher should encourage the trial of a variety of activities even if the student appears somewhat hesitant to attempt the unknown. In all cases, however, the supervising teacher must assume responsibility for judging the appropriateness of the activity and for requiring modification of those deemed threatening to instructional and/or operational security. The supervising teacher cannot abrogate this legal responsibility just because the student teacher has submitted a written proposal which later may prove to have been inadequate. It would be very easy to misinterpret these previous remarks as intention that the supervising teacher exercise undue restraint upon the activities and latitude of the student teacher. Such is not the case. Rather, supervising teachers must be aware of their responsibilities and exercise them. There is no implication that a listing of activities by the student teacher provides license to do whatever has been proposed. Neither is there intent that the supervising teacher forbid anything which deviates from activities as practiced by the supervising teacher. Here again is an opportunity for the professional supervising teacher to make decisions which best exemplify the nature of the process.

The college supervisor by virtue of his exposure to many different supervising teachers, student teachers and school settings can be an exceedingly valuable resource by providing suggestions which increase the variety of instructional activity. The college methods instructors and methods textbooks can also be helpful in this connection. An often overlooked and yet extremely important source of instructional activities involves observation of other teachers within the school. The supervising teacher can assist by being familiar with different instructional activity as exemplified by his colleagues within the building or school system, and further by directing the student teacher's observation to a variety of teaching styles. It is certainly not the college's expectations that every supervising teacher have knowledge of or be competent in the use of the total range of instructional activities, but it would seem reasonable that the collegiate institution can expect the supervising teacher to be aware of instructional activities beyond those which he himself uses and further to be of help to the student teacher in acquiring exposure to a variety.

Division of the activities whether they be pupil, teacher, or supervising teacher-oriented, into general and specific categories can be done. A detailing of the activities at the specific level is most necessary during the earliest stages of student teaching. The student teacher needs the reassurance of a virtual step-by-step scripting to overcome the butterflies of initial performances. As certain activities become automatic in the behavior patterns of the student teacher, these can be logically reduced to a simple word or two in the plan. At no stage, however, is it suggested that a student teacher's planning be reduced to the size of box frequently found in the "Teacher's Plan Book" which size permits only entries such as "Read pages 13-18" or "classroom discussion." The student teacher is hardly experienced enough to be able to translate these into a meaningful period of activity. Such entries are also so general that meaningful evaluation in the post-observation conferences between the student and supervising teacher is difficult.

Materials.

This third section is a simple listing of the materials that are needed in connection with the aforementioned activities and which in turn are designed to help accomplish the objectives. Once again it may be well to divide this section of the plan into those materials needed by the pupils and conversely those materials that the teacher will need in connection with the activities. Any materials needed by the pupils for a particular day which in turn must be brought to the classroom by them should appear on the previous day's plan. Supervising teachers bear responsibility for acquainting the student teacher with the nature and variety of material resources that are available for use not only within the classroom but also found in the various service agencies of the school or system. It is hoped that supervising teachers will immediately emphasize to the student teacher the necessity of beginning a collection of personal materials and resources for use after the student leaves the security of the supervising teacher's nest.

The student teacher by virtue of having recently completed the special methods courses may be familiar with a variety of instructional materials and resources beyond those known by the supervising teacher. Here is an instance where the student teacher can be an aid to the supervising teacher in terms of maintaining a recency of knowledge. The college supervisor, particularly if representative of the content being taught, should also be useful in this context. Once again, it is hoped that the initial plans of the student teacher will be quite specific in detail with respect to the material needed. Humorous and yet tragic stories are numerous about student teachers who assumed that because a chalkboard was in the room that chalk would be available, and that because a projector and film were ordered from the audio-visual department that a take-up reel would likewise be furnished. It is the supervising teacher's responsibility to insure that "because a nail in a shoe was missing, the war was lost" is not a factor in terms of the student teacher's initial instructional success.

A common characteristic of student teachers would appear to be that most of their planned activities begin with an assessment of the material resources available to them. There is and must be an obvious relationship between materials and activities. It is the supervising teacher's responsibility, however, to insure that the student teacher view the instructional activity as the primary consideration prior to the assessment of materials. And then further that the supervising teacher do all in his power to insure that the student teacher exercise creativity and resourcefulness in terms of materials' production which can implement the optimal instructional activity. Student teachers, on the other hand, must not be permitted to use the rationale that "If only I had available," as an excuse for not engaging in an activity that would be deemed most efficient. Student teachers will vary in their degree of resourcefulness. Supervising teachers must in connection with materials assume the responsibility for encouraging resourcefulness, if it does not pre-exist.

Problem Situation #17

An insistent ringing rouses the college supervisor at 2:30 a.m. He sleepily listens to John describe his first unit examination grading trauma. It seems that everyone has failed the test and further it just happens to be the gifted group. John is obviously concerned, questioning his own ability; but yet quite certain that he had planned and taught well.

Evaluation.

This fourth major section of any plan contains a description of the methods or techniques intended to evaluate the objectives as listed in section one of the plan. The basic purpose of this section is to provide evidence that the learning objectives have been realized at a level such that with some assurance the next plan may be begun. Once again this section may be divided into evaluations designed for pupils and description of activities designed to evaluate the teacher. It is suggested that both sections, if used, be further subdivided into those evaluation activities which might be classified as formal as well as informal. Formal evaluation of activities would include quizzes, examinations, homework, seatwork, measures of skills development, and any types of formalized verbal assessment such as spelling bees, etc. Informal evaluation activities would include question and answer techniques, or other such techniques by which the teacher tries to develop a sense of whether the pupils have learned. All formal evaluation devices or activities to be used should be included with the plan. This provides opportunity for the supervising teacher to assess the merits of the intended device or technique in advance and will do much to preclude pupil complaints of student teacher unfairness in terms of testing or evaluation. Informal techniques, though less structured, should be describable. Any informal technique which cannot be described in terms of its purpose and method must be subject to some suspicion.

Evaluation techniques as listed under the student teacher section will most commonly be implemented by the supervising teacher in his role as an instructional observer. Formalized varieties would include any observation instruments that are to be utilized. The chapter on observation techniques contains a rather comprehensive description of the variety of such techniques that are available to supervising teachers. Reliance on purely informal techniques by the supervising teacher leads frequently to the very generalized, "Well done," or "That was not a very good lesson today." There is no implication that supervising teachers do not or should not utilize informal evaluation techniques. Rather the rationale is that complete reliance upon this type is inadequate and most frequently will not provide the student teacher with the degree of assessment of his performance that he needs for growth and development. Making the supervising teacher evaluation activities a purposeful part of the plan will help insure that communication exists between the student and supervising teacher. It also clearly indicates that the supervising teacher has an important role to play in this team effort. Observation, at best, is a laborious and frequently boring task. Having reason and structure during the observation will help to insure that it is meaningful for both the supervising and student teacher.

The primary reason for including evaluation as a part of every plan is to insure that the student teacher views it as a continuous process, recognizes that learning must progress on a graduated basis, and most importantly provides him with a daily assessment of himself as a producer of pupil learning.

Assignment and Motivation.

This final section may be viewed as an optional part of a plan. It is suggested, however, that the student teacher in the earliest phases be required to write out completely the assignment for the pupils which will grow out of the lesson that has been described in the foregoing sections of the plan. This same section should also contain a description of the motivational techniques or devices that will be used by the student teacher in an attempt to induce successful completion of the assignment.

A most common failing of student teachers relates to an inability in the early stages to accurately predict student work load and the time necessary to complete assignments. Complaints on the part of the pupils with respect to assignment overload and complaints from parents with respect to assignments being inadequate are commonplace, as most experienced supervising teachers will testify. Criticisms that student teacher-made assignments were not clear or did not provide sufficient instruction for the successful completion of the assigned work are also commonplace. The requirement that the student teacher write out exactly the assignment will permit the supervising teacher to react from his experience base in terms of the adequacy and clarity of the assignment. Requiring the student teacher to describe his motivational techniques will also help insure that recognition is made of the variety of motivation techniques and help insure that the student teacher not constantly rely on only one or two types.

Making this section a part of each plan also helps insure a continuity of learning from day to day. The student teacher can hardly avoid thinking about the relationship of yesterday to today to tomorrow if he is required to complete this section. The specificness of this section may well be reduced as the student teacher demonstrates competence in this area. It is hoped, however, that it never becomes the type frequently found in teacher plan books, "Read pages 16-18." And further that motivation never relies solely upon, "And we'll have a quiz tomorrow."

SUMMARY

This chapter has tried to emphasize the importance of planning. It has attempted to clarify that a positive attitude with respect to the necessity for planning is more critical than the niceties of planning technique. No attempt was made, however, to minimize the importance of the individual team member's responsibilities, or to imply that techniques are not paramount to success. In fact, the majority of the presentation was devoted to these two factors. Nevertheless, the contention still remains that the greatest impediment to successful planning is that it is not being done. In a teacher training experience that is almost exclusively predicated upon growth and development, such neglect would be criminal.

CHAPTER SIX

OBSERVATION TECHNIQUES

> "It was about ten minutes before we regained our cab and drove back into Ross. Holmes still carried with him the stone which he had picked up in this wood.
> 'This may interest you, Lestrade,' he remarked, holding it out. 'The murder was done with it.'
> 'I see no marks.'
> 'There are none.'
> 'How do you know, then?'
> 'The grass was growing under it. It had lain there a few days. There was no sign whence it had been taken. It corresponds with the injuries. There is no sign of any other weapon.'
> 'And the murderer?'
> 'Is a tall man, left-handed, limps with the right leg, wears thick-soled shooting boots and a gray cloak, smokes Indian cigars, uses a cigar-holder, and carries a blunt penknife in his pocket. There are several other indications, but these may be enough to aid us in.our search.'
> Lestrade laughed. 'I am afraid that I am still a skeptic,' he said.
> 'Theories are all very well, but we have to deal with a hardheaded British jury.'
> 'Nous verrons,' answered Holmes calmly. 'You work with your own method, and I shall work mine.' "[1]

The famous deductive powers of Sherlock Holmes as illustrated in the above quotation are well-known to all murder mystery affectionadoes, and no matter how frequently employed never ceased to amaze Dr. Watson (and most of us). Holmes, however, did not appear able to improve significantly the good Doctor's observational prowess. But, then, Holmes was in the business of solving mysteries whereas the intent of this chapter is to improve your observational skills.

REASONS FOR OBSERVATION

Evaluation.

A premise that runs throughout this book is that learning is best accomplished when both the teacher and learner are aware of and have

---

[1] A. Conan Doyle, *Best of Sherlock Holmes: The Bascombe Valley Mystery* (New York: Grosset, n.d.).

accepted the objectives intended for achievement. Such an awareness and acceptance appears most critical to the improvement of both the observational process and its successful use in the development of a teacher trainee. For example, many trainees and their supervisors are seemingly aware of only a single purpose for observation; e.g., "evaluation," and as a consequence fear it, resist it, and do all in their power to make the observation either an example of excellence via a virtual scripting of instruction or a kind of contest designed to capture the observed at his worst. So long as evaluation is the primary reason for observation, even if an honest and open atmosphere prevails, deception must be recognized as a legitimate and logical interferent to awareness and acceptance of remedial weaknesses.

Evaluation as a reason for observation is both legitimate and necessary in the teacher training process, but its negative connotations must be recognized and minimized. At least three recent efforts in this direction would seem worthy of mention. First, the shift in grading practice from the artificial preciseness of the letter or number grade to a Pass/Fail or Satisfactory/Unsatisfactory arrangement has helped minimize the need to "nit-pick" in the attempt to finely differentiate. Second, increased direct involvement of the trainee throughout the preparation program in a wide variety of field experiences has improved the screening process so that the necessity for a "life or death" type of evaluation is not as critical as it once was when student teaching was literally the only screening device employed. Third, and most important, is the growing acceptance of the principle of self-evaluation as the only realistic and meaningful improvement process. To the extent that supervising teachers and college supervisors can structure the observational process so that it has meaning for the trainee in the development of his self-analysis skills, observation becomes a positive process that most trainees and supervisors can readily accept and eagerly use.

Growth and Development.

This second and more important reason for observation relates to its use in helping the trainee grow and develop during the field experience itself. The observational process itself needs to be seen as an instructional objective for any field experience. That is, all supervisors need to accept responsibility for helping the trainee develop his observational and self-analysis skills. This can provide the greatest potential for continued development on the part of the trainee once he has left the security and help of constant supervision.

The reason for observation is critical both in terms of acceptance by the trainee and usableness in modifying his instructional behavior.

As will be pointed out in Chapter 8, behavior modification is most easily accomplished when its approach and purpose are positive in nature. Observation will be more acceptable and effective if the supervising teacher and student trainee both view it as helping to furnish the basis for analysis and improvement rather than if evaluation is its prime purpose. Evaluation is certainly important and a prime responsibility of the supervisor, as will be discussed in Chapter 9; but it hardly need be the cause, justification, or reason for daily observations.

VARIETIES OF OBSERVATIONS

Just as it is important to recognize the basic reasons for observations, so is it necessary to realize the scope of observational opportunities. A variety of observational experiences seems necessary to present an accurate and realistic portrayal of the teaching profession. Obviously the extent and need of such experiences will vary from student to student. The student's own background, and particularly the extent to which he has been involved with field observations during the pre-student teaching program, are determining factors. This point, the determination of observational needs, too, is just one more reason why the communication process between student and supervisor is so critical. The good supervising teacher will constantly keep in mind that this training period probably represents the final opportunity for the trainee to engage in extended observations—particularly those that are guided and in which a supervisor can help the student develop his analytical skills.

Observations can be grouped in a number of ways. One of the simplest is to organize them in terms of the two prime responsibilities of teachers;

Figure 6:1 Observable *Instructional* Personnel

Instruction Related Observations:

—Of the supervising teacher or teachers

—Of other teachers (*same* grade level or subject area)

—Of other teachers (*other* grade levels or subjects areas)

—Of other student teachers

—Of self (the student teacher himself)

that is, in terms of instruction and activities. Organization in this fashion can help prevent the student from seeing education either as only the dispensing of knowledge or the socializing of the pupils. It will help also to remember that the prime reason for observation is the improvement of the trainee's instructional capacities. To the extent that his awareness and knowledge of the activities of teachers apart from instruction have a relationship to his instructional improvement, such observation can be justified. It is most critical that the supervising teacher knows what is being observed and the reasons for such observations so that help can be given in this analysis process.

Instruction-Related Observations

Observation of the supervising teacher(s) is undoubtedly the most common type done by the trainee during any part of his field experiences and most certainly so during the student teaching period. This is as it should be since the student needs the opportunity to observe a teacher over a span of time so the developmental relationship between a teacher and his learners can be observed. Such observations can also provide the supervising teacher the opportunity to illustrate good observational techniques in a non-threatening way by permitting the trainee to use these techniques and also to illustrate the self-analysis process through his own actions. It should be obvious that none of this can happen if the supervisor stops teaching the day the trainee walks into the room.

Observation of other teachers at the same grade or unit level or in the same subject area, if secondary, is critical if the supervising teacher is to avoid providing himself as the single model of instructional excellence. The same is true with respect to teachers at other grade levels or in other subject areas. Certainly we would not want to imply that only third grade or science teachers have all of the instructional competence, would we! Not only does observing teachers in other grades or subject areas provide the opportunity for instructional techniques acquisition, it also has meaning in terms of the content of such disciplines or levels and their possible relationship to that of the trainee. Most importantly, it gives the student a chance to see pupils react to teachers and instruction apart from his own particular interest. A most interesting and valuable technique is to suggest that the student teacher visit the other classes of the pupils he teaches. It frequently comes as a source of amazement to the trainee that the problem pupil for him is someone else's "All-Star" and vice versa. There is no better way to initiate self-analysis on the part of the trainee than to couch it in terms of comparing the different results attained with pupils and then asking that most important question: "Why?"

Observing a variety of teachers and/or content areas is most important in the early stages of the pre-student teaching training program to help the trainee identify his future level or subject area. Many supervising teachers would be surprised at the process, or lack thereof, by which a student teacher finds himself at the primary level or a prospective teacher of French. Most students appear to decide on the basis of either a strong success factor in a subject area or an equally strong or stronger identification with a previous teacher. In either case, surprisingly little exploration or conscious analysis has taken place. But then, how did you decide? And shouldn't there be a better way?

A relatively new observational technique[2] involves the concept of peer supervision—in this case, a student teacher interacting with other student teachers. Such observations have obvious implications for peer support in a less threatening relationship than the usual supervisor-student arrangement. Such observational and analysis opportunities are conditioned, however, on a concentration of student teachers and is another valid argument that can be advanced for such placements.

Observation by the student of himself as a teacher was only a dream just a few years ago. Modern technology now provides several tools which can capture sight and sound and recreate it for our personal examination. In addition, the fields of psychology and counseling now offer usable techniques of inspection and introspection, which if known, can be taught to and used by student teachers. These media and techniques will be explored later in this chapter.

Figure 6:2 Observable *Activity* Personnel

Activity Related Observations:

—Of pupils (clubs, organizations, playground, lunch, etc.)

—Of teachers (meetings, organizations, lunch, lounge, etc.)

—Of administrators, counselors, consultants, custodians, nurses, etc.

—Of community groups and agencies, parents, school board, etc.

[2] Hans Olsen, Chandler Barbour and Daniel Michalak, *The Teaching Clinic: A Team Approach to the Improvement of Teaching,* Association of Teacher Educators Bulletin #30 (Washington, D.C.: The Association, 1971).

Activity-Related Observations

Activity-related observations are frequently overlooked by both the supervising teacher and the trainee for potential relationship to the development and growth of the trainee. This is not to say that either supervisors or students consciously avoid involvement with either student or teacher/administrator/community activities, but rather that rarely do they seem to approach this type of observation in the same purposeful observation/learning/modification sequence as they do with those observations related to instruction. A wise supervising teacher will be aware that student teachers are only vaguely, at best, attuned to the purposes of activities; very sensitive to what they see and hear teachers do and say; and most apt to misinterpret the typical repartee of the faculty lounge or the boiler room. Student teachers and other types of trainees need your help in understanding the relationship of these various kinds of activities to the instructional process and the purposes of the schools. Fortunately, both supervisor and student can be simultaneously involved as observers in most of the activities listed. Remember that realism demands that students be involved in what teachers do. Not only do they not need shielding or protection from these kinds of activities, they need help in becoming involved. More importantly, they need help in understanding and making use of them.

Problem Situation #18

Mr. M. tells the visiting college supervisor that he has been informed by the representatives of the local teachers' association that conditions under which teachers may be observed, by whom, and for what reasons are to be included in the negotiation package for next year. Mr. M. wonders whether the college would like to be represented at the negotiation sessions inasmuch as all of their teacher education students are required to observe.

There are obvious problems involved in both arranging and implementing observations for the student teacher or trainee. Which teachers or activities to observe? For what? When? Who should make the contacts and requests? How do both the supervising and student teacher observe someone else at the same time? How can the supervising teacher be of help in the analysis process if he has not observed with the trainee? How can peers, administrators, community persons, etc., be prepared so that they understand the purposes of the observations and accept them and are not threatened by them? The questions are many and the solutions to most are not perfect or easy. Some techniques will be suggested in the remainder of this chapter. The college supervisor should be of some assistance; but for the most part, the supervising teacher personally will need to devise his own solutions. In this instance, much as Holmes suggested in the opening quotation, knowing the problems goes a long way toward finding a solution.

BASIC OBSERVATION PRINCIPLES

It would seem helpful to be aware of and make use of certain basic principles so that all types of observations can be made most valuable. Nothing particularly unique characterizes these principles. They are those of any good learning situation. The primary reason for listing and describing them is simply because they are so basic they are frequently overlooked. This is another proposition espoused by Holmes, "The obvious is so often such that it is ignored." The principles will be organized and presented in a time-use sequence; that is, those that have Pre or During or Post observation application.

Pre-Observation Principles.

The best observations are:

(1) those that have a specific purpose or purposes that are known to both the observer and observee. The best, or highest order of purposes will deal with the "whys" as opposed to the "hows." "Hows" usually result in little more than replication or modeling behavior, although nothing here suggests that such action is necessarily bad. The "whys," because of the depth of understanding usually generated, can provide for options of recourse, and as such, permit the trainee to develop a style unique to and compatible with his own individuality.

(2) pre-planned and organized. This means that conditions of time and place should be decided in advance and that all parties to them should be aware and acceptant of the conditions. There is something to be said for the unannounced observation, particularly for the trainee who may be unduly apprehensive; but if improvement is to be the name of the game, then the subject needs the opportunity to perform at his highest level. By the same token, advance scheduling of observations can help remove the crutch that all supervisors have heard so often,

"If only you had been here yesterday," or, "This is my bad class."

(3) those in which both the observer and the observed are aware of the purpose of the observation. As will be elaborated in the next section, "Observable Components," prior identification of purpose is most important if the observation is to involve any type of post-instructional conference. The value of permitting the student teacher to help determine the purpose of the observation should be obvious if the true intent is the maximizing of self-analysis. This student determination of what is to be the focus of the observation has particular merit in the early stages of the experience when *any* observer for *any* reason is threatening. What the student initially selects may not have much real instructional implication, but rest assured that to him it will be meaningful and most importantly usually not threatening. There will be plenty of time to work into the critical items. Keep in mind that one can only risk failure who has achieved a certain degree of success.

(4) those in which the supervisor exercises leadership and responsibility. It is expecting too much to ask or require the trainee to set all of the times, places, and purposes of observation. Few of us would schedule observations any more frequently than our students under the same set of circumstances. Likewise absenting oneself from the classroom for the reason that the student needs a chance to try his own wings may appear noble, and not infrequently appealing to certain students; but the plain fact is that what is not observed can hardly furnish a basis for the best type of analytical conference. This is certainly not to imply that the supervising teacher should never leave the room, but rather that recognition must be made that absence is not equatable with observation unless certain conditions prevail. These specialized conditions and techniques will be further discussed in the next section of this chapter.

During-Observation Principles.

These observations are those:

(1) so conducted that neither it (the process) nor the observer himself become a contributing factor to the success or failure of what is observed. There are many reasons why the supervisor should not interrupt or intrude upon the student when that student

is the one primarily responsible for the instruction. It also implies that the location and actions of the observer must be as unobtrusive and non-distracting as possible. This may be difficult to accomplish in the early stages of the student teaching; but if an honest effort is made, the problem should soon resolve itself.

(2) that provide for objective and accurate recording of behavior. Memory for most observers is a very poor substitute for the use of some type of recording instrument or technique. Not only does the use of such instruments or devices permit accurate retention, but it also helps provide a specific focus which can then provide the basis for later conferencing and analysis. A conflicting interpretation of what was done and what was seen has been the cause for more than one disagreement between student teachers and supervisors. Hopefully the description in the next section concerning ways that observations can be made more objective and accurate will help to minimize such disagreements. It might be pointed out here, however, that no perfect solutions are available since even reality itself is subject to interpretation at the analysis stage. Since this is true, it would appear even more critical that great care be exercised during the observation itself so that subjectivity and inaccuracy do not cloud the problem at a point where they can be controlled. In other words, disagreements can be expected at the interpretation (the post-observation conference analysis) stage which focuses on the "Why." It is critical that the "What Happened" stage (the during-observation) be arranged to insure maximum objectivity and accuracy.

Post-Observation Principles.

The best observations result in:

(1) some type of action involving the trainee. Observations which culminate in memories or notes acquired by the observer and which are not shared with the student teacher are apt to be disconcerting to the student and also very clearly indicate that evaluation, not growth, was the real purpose for the observation. This post-observation action on the part of the observed need not always consist of a two or three (if the college supervisor is included) person conference. Action might also include the student viewing himself on video tape, listening to himself on audio-tape, reading the notes, or comments of the observer,

or simply engaging in retrospective self-analysis predicated on what he remembers. These techniques have varying levels of value which will be further discussed in the next section.

(2) analysis on the part of both the supervising teacher and the student in terms of the purposes for which the observation was made. Such analysis is necessary if the supervisor is truly interested not only in the present growth of his trainee, but also concerned about the future self-development of that person. Self-analysis is a process that must be taught, learned, and practiced.

OBSERVABLE COMPONENTS

Purposes and principles are necessities if the quality of observation is to be improved, but techniques (the "Hows") are also critical to the success of the process. Some readers may question the amount of emphasis on purposes and principles which has preceded this section, but an understanding of and commitment to improving the observational process is the absolutely critical stage which must precede any in-depth analysis or use of specific techniques.

Certain techniques have already been described in the presentation on purposes and principles. Many others exist. The discussion of them can be organized in a number of ways; e.g., in terms of machinery, aids, and instruments; in terms of the actions of the people involved—the observer and the observed; in terms of the specific technique used—its directness or indirectness, etc.

Problem Situation #19

A troubled college supervisor wonders how to respond to a request just made by the building principal for him to share his observation notes with the selection and tenure committee.

What is to be Observed?

Irrespective of the method of organization, virtually all decisions with respect to the value or use of a technique(s) must depend on the answer to the question, "What is to be observed?" or at an even more obscure level, "What is observable?" The immediate response to such questions is apt to be, "What does it all mean?". Even more critically, it often results in a superficiality of observation and the comments resulting from it. Most instructional and activity situations are so complex and comprised of so many variables that an unstructured observation usually results in one of two actions. Either the observer is literally overwhelmed by the complexity, and as a consequence deals in generalities, "That was a good lesson today," or tends to focus on single, usually low-level variables, "The chalk squeaked," or "Your writing on the board went downhill," or "Your voice needs to be louder." These comments are not intended to suggest that trainees do not need generalized impressions, "That was a good lesson," or specific constructive criticism, "The chalk squeaked"; but rather that if the observer is not aware of the components that comprise what is observable, the end result may be the old forest or trees syndrome.

What can you observe? The answer to this is obviously dependent upon the observational situation. Not all of the following are necessarily present in every individual class or activity session, but their totalities do represent the forest. For example, as shown in Figure 6:3, the observable components might be organized in different ways.

The critical decision lies not so much with the choosing of which one of the four constructs to use (they actually have virtually all components in common and differ only in primary focus), but rather in the recognition that each set contains separate parts. If all are used, it will help insure both specificity and totality of coverage. Knowledge of the components is also essential to the decisions concerning how, who, and when to utilize specific observational techniques. For example, the selection and use of an interaction analysis instrument for the affective dimension has little direct implication for the cognitive domain. Likewise, a college supervisor who is a generalist rather than a specialist in a

Figure 6:3 Observable Components

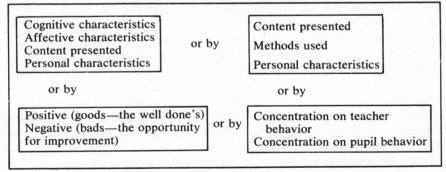

specific content area is likely to be less effective as a helpful observer with respect to a content area other than his own. Or focusing observation and analysis on pupil behavior in the early days of student teaching is apt to be less than meaningful to the trainee who first has to survive as a person/teacher. Or the decision to use an audio tape recording for observation and analysis of the student's personal characteristics may well overlook or ignore critical non-verbal factors. The key questions in terms of observational technique selection are really the same as for the selection of any instructional technique or aid. For what purpose? What can it contribute? What are its limitations? How can it best be used?

SPECIFIC TECHNIQUES—SIMPLE TO COMPLEX

Observation techniques are as old as man himself and as modern as science and research can provide. As simple as memory and written anecdotal records and as complex as some instructional analysis systems which may require many hours of training and practice prior to their use.

Memory.

Trying to remember all that transpired during an observational period may appear overwhelming or even futile when one realizes that the memories of two people, supervisor and trainee, must be trusted. The task of memory training is difficult, but in the absence of any substitute method of totally recording all that happens, there would appear to be no way to eliminate a heavy dependence on it. There are no particular secrets involved in improving memory. If the rationale just presented for the use of memory has been accepted, the first step toward improvement has been made. The next is to attempt total recall (exact actions, whole conversations, complete physical descriptions). Try it first for only brief time periods and in situations which involve only a few persons. Try making it a game with the student trainee. Identify a bit of the period that both of you will try to remember absolutely. Then later verbally compare what is remembered. The first several trials will be frustrating, and both of you may wonder if the same piece of action was observed. Rather quickly, however, both of you will begin to sound like tape recorders. One of the side advantages to this effort at memory improvement is the extent to which forced attention to the objective action in a classroom or activity helps eliminate or at least minimize subjective differences in interpretation.

You may never reach the level of interpretation of a Sherlock Holmes, but hopefully you won't always remain at the always amazed and frequently befuddled level of a Doctor Watson either. There are "tricks of the trade" in the memory improvement game—using mnemonic or associative techniques, etc. A variety of books at the paperback counter or the library can provide these. The prime necessity, though, is simply a desire to improve and practice, practice, practice. The best existent evidence of success are the many college supervisors who have amazed supervising and student teachers with what appears to be almost total recall. They are living proof of what intent and practice can produce.

Problem Situation #20

The college supervisor on an earlier visit had suggested anecdotal recording by the supervising teacher as a means of avoiding the student teacher's complaint of too infrequent and too generalized reactions. After reading one week's anecdotal recording and noting excellent descriptions of what had occurred, but still only generalized "well-dones" or "could be improved" comments, he ponders what to suggest next.

Anecdotal Recording.

This is an attempt to retain impressions by writing down major portions of what transpires as it happens and usually at the time it occurs. Major difficulties with this technique are that usually so much is happening so fast that any attempt at completeness of recording either forces attention on the recording effort and detracts from the observing or the observer finds himself falling farther and farther behind the ever-moving action. The next step is usually an abandonment of the effort. Improvements in the use of this technique consist of deciding in advance to use it on only small portions of the observation period; e.g., first five minutes of the period, the assignment giving portion, or distribution of materials period. Devising and using a coding or shorthand type or recording is also helpful. Unless standardized, however, this may necessitate a good deal of translation before it has much meaning for the trainee. A prime advantage to the anecdotal type record is that it is complete enough to mean something if examined at a later time. A sequence of these collected over a period of time can help in the interpretation of growth and development. It is doubtful if memory, no matter how well developed, can ever serve such a purpose.

Split Half Technique.

This type of recording usually consists of only brief comments (just enough to jog the memory of both the student and supervising teacher) or more frequently of questions concerning why something was done. The technique can be used for focused observations, but most frequently is employed throughout an observation period to record anything that might be thought of interest or necessity. The technique derives its name from the recording of the supervisor's comments or questions on one-side of the page and allowing use of the other half for the student's response or reaction. A stenographer's notepad is ideally designed for this use. The technique requires little or no prior preparation. It provides continuous dialogue between supervisor and the student—rather like a chain letter. It permits the student a chance to think about and respond to the comments and questions—digestion time is frequently lacking in conferences held immediately after an observation. And certainly it does provide a diary of progress. The prime disadvantages are that though the recordings are rather constant and chronological, they tend to be randomized and rarely concentrate on either all the parts or the totality— the trees are there all right, but individual ones may be overlooked and even worse, the boundaries of the forest may not be found at all. This technique is a good complementary type; that is, it works well as an easily used daily technique whereas some ways (techniques) yet to be discussed either have limited daily value or would be cumbersome if attempted that frequently.

Numeric Tallying.

All of us at some time have recorded the number of "ahs" used by a speaker, or the number of times a throat was cleared, or a particular pupil called upon or reprimanded, or the number of minutes it took to call the roll. We may even have established a numeric rating system for the quality of the instructor's jokes or the attractiveness of the dress worn on different days. Whether we realized it at the time or not, we were trying not only to record actions or behavior, but also to quantify and objectify that action or behavior. The technique is appropriate for those things that lend themselves to counting and about which there is rather common agreement concerning their existence or happening. Trying to count, or weigh, or assign a quality value is not quite so simple for subjective or interpretive items; particularly when explanation is attempted or comparison is made with another person's judgment. Observations which focus on the use of numeric tallying also appear more final and definitive than is warranted simply because the technique is so specific. Tallies may provide, "The facts, nothing but the facts," but rarely do such listings provide anything more than clues in dealing with the "Whys" and "So Whats." A Holmes may have been able to make the summation of evidence always equal the answer, but few of us have this talent and the danger is that if most of us try, we only succeed in identifying the wrong causes or killers (and even worse, we may feel justified in so doing).

Instructional Analysis Systems.

The structured recording of classroom verbal interaction appears old if the earliest work of H. H. Anderson and John Withal in the 1930's and '40's is examined. It was not, however, until the efforts of Ned Flanders in the middle 1950's that the movement began to have implications for and gain use-acceptance for the analysis of teacher behavior. Interestingly enough from our perspective, most of the early testing and research efforts involved field testing with supervising and student teachers. These early efforts focused on the analysis of verbal interaction between such teachers and their pupils in a classroom setting. The limitations of such systems because of their concentration on the verbal and affective dimensions and the attractiveness of the approach as a research and improvement tool resulted in a proliferation of authors and similiar systems. The Second Edition of *Mirrors of Behavior,*[3] a two-volume publication of Research for Better Schools, Inc., analyzes seventy-nine published systems. This publication is the single best source available for obtaining not only a description of virtually all of the available systems, but also a comparative analysis of each. The editors have attempted analysis in terms of seven criteria:

1. Settings in Which the System Is Used
2. Subject of the Observation
3. Number of Subjects Observed
4. Uses Reported by Author
5. Data Collection and Coding Methods and Personnel
6. Category Dimension of the System
7. Coding Units

It is interesting to note that in the two years since the publication

[3] Anita Simon and E. Gil Boyer, Editors, *Mirrors for Behavior II: An Anthology of Observation Instruments* (Philadelphia: Research for Better Schools, Inc., 1970).

of the first edition of *Mirrors* that the creators of such instructional observation systems expanded the nature of their use. This is apparent since in 1967 the editors found it necessary to use only four categories to define the "Dimensions of the Systems" being analyzed. The number of categories was expanded to seven in the second edition and are as follows: (1) Affective, (2) Cognitive, (3) Psychomotor or Location, (4) Activity, (5) Content (work process, procedures, routine, control), (6) Sociological Structure (roles, who to whom, etc.), and (7) Physical Environment. Several of these, notably (4), (5), and (6), have direct implication for the three remaining sections of this Specific Techniques topic.

A recent publication[4] of the *Association of Teacher Educators* is extremely valuable for a concise and easily understandable overview of the field. It is a very good beginning source to find whether one wants to "dig deeper." In addition to the review of the interaction analysis movement, the publication contains other sections which focus on classroom observation systems used in the preparation process and supervisory conferences and the implications that such systems hold for them.

Simply knowing of the availability of such techniques and sources of information about them, however, does not solve the "use problem." Flanders, quite literally the father of the modern movement, pointed out in an article in 1964, reprinted in 1967,[5] some precautions, which are just as valid today, regarding the use of interaction analysis in situations involving student teachers:

"First, no interaction analysis data should be collected unless the person observed is familiar with the entire process and knows its limitations.

Second, the questions to be answered by inspecting the matrix should be developed before the observation takes place.

Third, value judgments about good and bad teaching behavior are to be avoided. Emphasis is given to the problem being investigated so that cause-and-effect relationships can be discovered.

---

[4] Norma Furst, J. T. Sandefur and Alex A. Bressler, and Donald P. Johnston, *Interaction Analysis: Selected Papers,* Association of Teacher Educators Research Bulletin #10 (Washington: The Association, 1971).

[5] E. J. Amidon and J. B. Hough, Editors, *Interaction Analysis: Theory, Research, and Application* (Reading, Mass: Addison-Wesley Publishing Co., 1967), p. 293. Perhaps the best and most complete single reference source concerning the total interaction analysis field.

Fourth, a certain amount of defensive behavior is likely to be present at the initial consultations; it is something like listening to a tape recording for the first time.

Fifth, a consultation based on two observations or at least two matrices helps to eliminate value judgments or at least control them. Comparisons between the matrices are more likely to lead to principles."

The first caution is of interest because it mandates a thorough training process for both the supervising and student teacher. A description by Flanders of the training process necessary[6] makes very clear that simply reading about the system and its techniques is not sufficient to its use. Most teacher preparation institutions have personnel available who can provide such training. Why not inquire?

The second caution is of interest, if for no other reason than because it so closely resembles an observation principle stated earlier in this chapter, "Purpose must be pre-established."

The third precaution is apt to discourage some thoughtful supervising teachers. They are likely to wonder whether it is not contradictory to the very task and responsibility they have accepted—that is, making value judgments concerning the "good or bad teaching behavior" of the student teacher assigned to them. The statement is actually more concerned with the avoidance of prevalue judgments which could have the effect of limiting trials of differing teaching behaviors and the implication that a single, most acceptable model of teaching behavior exists, than it is with a seeming acceptance of "anything goes."

The purpose of this particular section has been to describe what many teacher educators regard as a most valuable improvement tool. A tool, incidentally, that utilizes observation and analysis as its primary media. Any teacher or administrator who is truly serious about the supervision business needs to know more about these techniques. There is simply no way, however, that a book such as this can provide all of the knowledge of and training in such systems that is needed to use them successfully. A more detailed presentation of several of the systems and their uses will be made in Chapter 9.

The types of written recordings just described have ranged from simplistic, literally random notations, to highly complex systems of instructional analysis. The very complexity and great numbers of these latter systems are apt to give the impression that there is nothing that happens in a classroom which cannot be recorded by using them. Flanders himself, however, points out that

[6] *Ibid.*, pp. 158-166.

"Interaction analysis is a specialized research procedure that provides information about only a few of the many aspects of teaching. It is an analysis of spontaneous communication between individuals, and it is of no value if no one is talking, if one person talks continuously, or if one person reads from a book or report. Unless additional records are kept, the following kinds of information will be ignored—right, wrong, good, or bad content information—whatever is being discussed, the variety of instructional materials being used; the various class formations during learning activities; the preparation of the teacher as revealed by lesson plans; and anything else not directly revealed by verbal communication. Of the total complex called 'teaching,' interaction analysis applies only to the content-free characteristics of verbal communication."[7]

Because the previously described techniques have either no, or only limited, direct application to subject matter, methods, and personality the next three sections are offered.

Problem Situation #21

John A., a student teacher in an open-space primary room, tells his college supervisor that the subject matter being taught is not important—that socialization should be the primary objective and that only the degree to which this is successfully accomplished should be obseived. A question about whether the supervising teacher agrees with this premise elicits the response, "We haven't talked about that yet."

Subject-Matter Analysis Instruments and Techniques.

The nature and level of content taught varies greatly because of the age, prior experience, and intellectual level of the learner. Thus, though American history is a rather common offering at the elementary, junior high, and senior high school levels, the same criteria of appropriateness would hardly be applicable in all three situations. A particular curricular emphasis; e.g., Black American History, would also have an effect upon an analysis of content appropriateness. The same would be true if a particular methodological approach were being used. Last, but certainly

[7] *Ibid.,* pp. 218–219.

not least, are the rather obvious implications that the education and experience of the teacher with respect to content might have on what is taught. For these and several other reasons, few instruments are available to help record the content proficiency of the trainee. Several of the professional associations which have content as their focus; e.g., social studies, mathematics, English, foreign language, etc.; do have analysis scales or instruments that can prove useful. The supervising teacher will need to contact the appropriate association to obtain its listing of such available materials. One of the limitations which will become quickly apparent is that what is available tends to treat of the nature of content as opposed to the student teachers' use of it. Even so, contact with the professional associations could prove useful.

A perhaps shocking but certainly true fact is that most college supervisors will be of little direct help in this area. Most are "generalists" and unless he has preparation in what is taught, probably the best he can do is to recommend someone back at the college who can provide the particular content competence help needed.

What this really means is that for the most part the supervising teacher alone is expected and required to be the primary judge of whether or not the trainee has sufficient subject matter competence to be a teacher.

Figure 6:4 Subject Matter Analysis Factors

Is the content being observed
—consistent with the course and curriculum objectives?
—appropriate for the learning and maturity level of the learners?
—presented in terms of its sequential relationship to the content that has preceded and will follow it?
—organized so that it has internal consistency?
—taught with appropriate vocabulary? Appropriate to the learners? Correctly pronounced? Correctly defined and used?
—accurate?
—so taught as to acknowledge options or different interpretations, if appropriate?
—being taught with a depth of understanding beyond the textbook of the learners?
—supplemented by aids, examples, and illustrations?
—taught to show relationships to other content or areas?
—taught at the level of (1) facts, (2) skills, (3) concepts, (4) attitudes, (5) appreciations? Are all levels incorporated in the learning if appropriate?
—taught as an end in itself or as a problem solving tool?

The responsibility may be frightening, but it must be assumed. Hopefully the series of questions to be posed next will be some help in the formulation of a personal observational recording instrument, and further that it can serve as the basis for many fruitful conferences between supervisor and trainee with respect to subject matter strengths and weaknesses.

Undoubtedly supervising teachers can add a number of content analysis factors to this listing. Consideration of such items and the careful observing and recording of them will certainly help the student trainee focus more specifically on content strengths and weaknesses. A careful attention to recording and analysis can also be of assistance to the student in terms of recommending future study, which could complement strength and which might help remediate weakness.

Instructional Methods Analysis Instruments and Techniques.

Quite recent in origin are observations specifically directed to an examination of how well the student teacher either utilizes the appropriate method or the degree to which the appropriate method(s) is implemented. Attention to discernible parts of the teaching act literally began with the work of Dwight Allen and his associates in connection with the development of micro-teaching as a training process. Though they were most emphatic that the components identified not be construed as constituting the sum total of the teaching act, their work did focus the attention of educators on the necessity of examining the teaching act in terms of identifiable elements. Something more than coincidence (such as the efforts of these individuals) contributed to the inclusion of "content and method" areas in the development of several of the more recently derived instructional analysis systems.

A major problem is that no generally acceptable definition of what constitutes "good or bad" method is available. This is frustrating, as pointed out by Sandefur and Bressler[8] when they wrote, "The paradox of classroom observation systems is that, while the profession now has the tools for quantifying teaching behavior, there are no generally accepted criteria for what constitutes effective teaching behavior." The problem exists, but there should be no attempt by either supervising teachers or college supervisors to evade or compromise methods' oriented observations because of a lack of definitive definition. Rather it would seem even more critical that communication take place to identify the characteristics of method that are mutually agreeable and hence mutually observable and capable of evaluation. The work of Allen, previously mentioned, in identifying components of the teaching act (establishing

[8] Furst, *op. cit.*, p. 31.

set, cueing, etc.) and the work of Smith and Meux[9] which resulted in an observation scale, *Study of the Logic of Teaching,* which defined teaching as: (1) Defining, (2) Describing, (3) Designating, (4) Stating, (5) Reporting, (6) Substituting, (7) Evaluating, (8) Opining, (9) Classifying, (10) Comparing and Contrasting, (11) Conditional Inferring, (12) Explaining, and (13) Directing and Managing Classroom; certainly provide a starting point for any supervising teacher or college supervisor who is interested in observations specifically oriented to instructional methods. These sources plus two previously mentioned, *Mirrors of Behavior* and the *ATE Research Bulletin #10,* and a publication of the NEA[10] provide descriptions of observational systems that are presently available to provide some foundation for initial efforts in this direction.

The teacher's or supervisor's examination of the previously mentioned sources will quickly indicate, however, that much of what is most helpful will of necessity need to be self-designed. This is particularly true if the method has a specific orientation; such as, open-space, individualized instruction, team teaching, inquiry, or discovery. An identification of the objectives and characteristics of the specific method or approach by the "team," once done, should then rather easily be translatable into an observation instrument that can be used to determine to what degree the student teacher has successfully implemented the method or approach. To the extent that components of the approach; i.e., defining, or asking higher order questions, or individualizing assignments, are a part of existent observational systems, it would seem expedient for the "team" to make use of these portions. For this to happen, however, it is obvious that they must be aware of both the nature of the method or approach they are using and the various published systems that may have implication for their observational efforts. Responsibility for the latter identification might well rest with the college supervisor and again might constitute a significant portion of an in-service program designed to improve supervisory competence.

[9]B. Othanel Smith and Milton O. Meux, *A Study of the Logic of Teaching,* U.S. Department of Health, Education, and Welfare, Office of Education, Cooperative Research Project No. 258. (Urbana, Ill.: Bureau of Educational Research, College of Education, University of Illinois, 1962).

B. Othanel Smith and others, *A Study of the Strategies of Teaching,* U.S. Department of Health, Education, and Welfare, Office of Education, Cooperative Research Project No. 1640. (Urbana, Ill.: Bureau of Educational Research, College of Education, University of Illinois, 1967).

[10]Department of Instruction and Professional Development, Program, and Performance Evaluation Team, NEA, *Evaluation Systems for Education: Descriptive Abstracts* (Washington: The Association, 1973).

The NEA publication previously described contains a description[11] of a rather new approach to the problem of trying to define the teacher's instructional job. It presents *33 Roles for Teachers and Pupils in the Classroom* and would appear, though it does not order them, to at least provide a compendium from which some local determination could be made.

The best way to describe the problem might be to once again quote from Sandefur and Bressler[12] who summarized it as follows:

"A major challenge of the next decade will be to develop more unanimity in the profession as to what constitutes effective teaching behavior and to develop the categories for observation systems which both quantify and qualify these behaviors."

The problem for any conscientious supervising teacher is very real. The help presently available is minimal. The contribution that such teachers can make to the solution of the problem is great.

Personality Characteristics Analysis Instruments and Techniques.

If the reader has detected a lack of established definition of what constitutes appropriate subject matter and methods and also a lack of available measuring instruments, he made a correct assumption. If the previous discussions left him somewhat confused and uncertain, then this section should add to both conditions.

The personality of the teacher affects the classroom climate and the degree to which pupils learn. This point has been so well researched and, in addition, is so apparent that it needs no literature citations. The problem lies not so much with concern over whether personality is a legitimate observation characteristic, but rather with trying to establish those personality characteristics that most directly influence learning. One approach has been to state that all personality components are important and hence the list reads like the Girl Scout Handbook: kind, courteous, loyal, obedient, cheerful, helpful, friendly, etc., etc., etc. This approach seems to have three major flaws. First, it is so global that its sheer magnitude discourages even beginning observation, analysis, and evaluation. Second, it makes no attempt to discriminate between those variables which might be most critical to learning. And third,

[11] *Ibid.*, pp. 31–32.

[12] Furst, *op. cit.*, p. 31.

it so closely resembles perfection that literally no one can achieve it; at least in this life. Such an approach also appears predicated on the assumption that these characteristics are appropriate for all learners. Just as individual learners require individualized learning activities and materials best suited to their individual learning needs and capacities; so would it seem logical that individual learners have need for differing personality characteristics on the part of their teachers. This approach could be misinterpreted as meaning that whatever the personality of the student teacher it must be accepted since it will be good for some learners. Such is not the premise. Certain personality characteristics are, however, firmly enough established by research and experience that they at least furnish a beginning place for observation.

Such characteristics as: being positive, liking young people, caring for individuals, respecting individuals' rights and opinions, and exhibiting "openness," are commonly accepted as making a difference in how and whether pupils learn. A workable approach would be for the supervising and student teacher, and perhaps the college supervisor, to compile their own list of these characteristics and then describe what evidence will indicate whether the student teacher exemplifies the characteristic. This process will force cooperative examination and agreement on what is deemed acceptable, and further identify those behaviors which will be observed, analyzed, and evaluated.

Once, again, supervisors will find few published instruments available. Certainly none exists that can do the whole job. A number of the instructional analysis systems are oriented to the "affective domain," and these should be examined for the contributions they can make to an analysis of how the student teacher and his pupils relate to each other. The *Mirrors* and *ATE Research Bulletin #10* and a publication of the Association for Supervision and Curriculum Development[13] can provide assistance in this initial survey effort. It is hoped that supervising teachers will not become overly discouraged by the limited amount of help available in these latter three areas. Hopefully, they will regard their responsibility as being even greater and make the truly professional contribution that the on-site supervisor makes. Only at the classroom level are decisions of what subject matter, materials, and personality appropriate since these decisions are predicated on the needs of the individual learners within that classroom. The professionals, then, will recognize these as their observation responsibilities and do something about them.

---

[13] Walcott H. Beatty, Editor, *Improving Educational Assessment and An Inventory of Measurers of Affective Behavior* (Washington: Association for Supervision and Curriculum Development, 1969).

MEDIA AS OBSERVATIONAL TOOLS

The previous sections of this chapter focused on the use of various techniques which can be used by the supervisor. Many require the supervisor and/or student trainee to use some type of aid to assist in the retention of what has been observed so that the post-instrumental analysis and evaluation can have as objective a focus as possible. If done, such conferences will then be able to concentrate on "why" something was done rather than "what" was done.

Single Sensory Aids.

Aids which involve only a single sense—sight, sound, taste, touch, and smell—such as still cameras, silent motion picture cameras, audio tape recorders, charts, diagrams, analysis instruments, and typed lesson or activity scripts are examples of this category. It will require some ingenuity on the part of the supervisor to devise aids which feature taste, touch, or smell! Most of the single sensory aids are intended to be "memory joggers" rather than complete replicators of the total experience. Only the silent motion picture and audio tape aids have the facility for total capture, and even then if used singly, present only one-half of the experience observed. If used together, they become multi-sensory and belong in the next section.

Single sensory aids such as seating charts, grouping arrangements, or pupil response listings can be easily constructed and used by the observer for such purposes as indicating physical movements of the student teacher, numbers and levels of pupil responses, interaction between teacher and pupils, etc. There should be awareness and agreement between the student and supervising teacher, in advance, of what will be observed and how it will be tallied. There is nothing quite so disconcerting to the student teacher as to see an observer making multiple marks for some unknown purpose. There is no reason for not informing the student, in advance, of the specific things to be observed. After all, is it not our purpose to predicate analysis on the best that the student can do rather than upon the discovery of the worst!

Most of the valuable single sensory aids just described will be locally derived and produced. Published or commercially available analysis instruments are available as parts of established instructional analysis systems. Some of their coding and recording techniques are quite unique and the supervisor may find it possible to adapt some of these techniques to his local use.

The audio tape recorder has the facility for preserving the complete sound of what is observed. Adequate sound recording may be somewhat difficult in most classrooms unless multiple microphones are used or the pupil grouping is rather radically modified. If such modifications are done, there may be some very real questions raised about how typical the performance was. In fact, the first several attempts may result in "performances!" Once again with this aid, as was true with those previously described, awareness and acceptance by the student teacher of the use of the audio tape recorder must be a part of the process. Unknown recording might serve some useful purpose, but its ethic is certainly questionable.

The use of the still camera has not been a very popular or useful observation tool because of the time lag between the taking of the picture and processing of the film. The fairly recent perfection of the Polaroid camera and its almost instant development of the picture holds an untapped supervisory potential. The relatively high cost of the camera and process may be reasons why greater use has not been made of this aid. It is hoped that soon such cameras will be seen and used in the classroom for daily observations in addition to the recording of the student teacher's final party.

Multi-Sensory Aids.

The sound motion picture has been available for many years. The expense of the needed equipment, film, and processing has prevented its use as a supervisory aid in virtually all situations that were not a part of funded research. The rather recent development and production of sound "home movie" type equipment now permits the school or college to invest quite inexpensively. The film processing time lag, however, is still a primary deterrent to its use for conferencing immediately following the filmed observation. A series of filmed observations, however, can be a valuable permanent record of development by the student. It is suggested that such a series will be more valuable if it has a pre-determined focus; such as, observing the student teacher at work with individual students or small groups than if it is just a series of "random captures" of the student teacher in action.

The video tape recorder is one of the most valuable observation tools ever developed. It is relatively inexpensive to purchase, quite portable, utilizes instantly available recreation of sight and sound, utilizes tape that may be re-used numerous times, and has an operation easily learned by anyone. The equipment is quite commonly found on college campuses. It is not uncommon for student teachers to have encountered it as a part of their on-campus microteaching experiences or in their methods courses. Many colleges and universities now require their student teachers to learn to operate this equipment just as they require operational ability in connection with the slide projector or motion picture projector. The student teacher in these instances will have the advantage of having experienced being filmed and analyzed, and hence will not require the several preview performances usually necessary to preclude the medium being regarded as a monster which reveals only bad faults.

Many college supervisors now travel with a VTR unit and possibly could be persuaded to leave it for the use of the supervising and student teacher. This may not be necessary since many schools also now own VTR equipment. It may not have been purchased with observation of student teachers in mind, but maybe the athletic or speech departments will permit you to borrow theirs! The concentration of numbers of student teachers in centers or clusters has also frequently resulted in the joint purchase of VTR units by the cooperating schools and universities.

Suggestions for the most profitable use of this aid include: pre-determine what is to be filmed (use it for focused observations); secure mutual, advance, student and supervising teacher agreement on purpose and procedures; use it frequently enough so that it does not condition either the instruction of the teacher or the learning behavior of the pupils; use it as a conferencing (analysis) tool rather than a curiosity; and require the student teacher to use it for self-analysis. Few, if any, aids have the potential for improving supervision that the video tape recorder has. What is needed now is a shift from its use as a research tool to the practical contributions it can make in the day-by-day growth and development of the student teacher.

SUMMARY

This chapter had attempted to give the reader an awareness of the potential value of observations, particularly as it emphasizes the importance of viewing observations as a growth and development technique. It established certain premises designed to improve observations by focusing upon the supervisory behaviors necessary before, during, and after actual instructional or activity observation. A variety of observational techniques and aids was also presented and analyzed.

The supervisory emphasis in all cases was on the importance of the supervising teacher's acceptance and implementation of his local determination responsibility. Few complete "ready-made" instruments or packages are available; and even if so, great doubt exists whether they will fit without some "alterations." The supervisory "team" will need to be aware of, accept responsibility for, and be the local "tailors."

CHAPTER SEVEN

Conferencing Techniques

> There is a current story on the perils of communication which runs like this. A man encounters a friend and says: "I hear your brother has just left Penn State and is living in the Park Central." The friend replies: "Well, that isn't quite the way it is. My brother has just left the State Pen and is living in Central Park."
>
> Obviously, then we want to know, not only whether we are being heard, but whether we are being understood. *Arthur Larson*

So, too, are there many perils of communication in the student teaching process. While usually not as severe as in the example above, the student teacher, supervising teacher, and college supervisor have many opportunities to misunderstand one another. It is equally important that these three key people in the student teaching process not only hear but clearly understand one another. Not only must a supervisor be able to decide which messages a student teacher should receive, he must also be able to find a way to effectively communicate these messages. This requires a well developed set of communication skills such as those already discussed in Chapter Three. It also requires a will on the part of those involved to "really" communicate with one another. This chapter presents some of the important concepts concerning conferencing techniques.

Definition of a Conference.

The word "conference" implies that two or more persons are "conferring" with one another. One might define a conference as an "Interchange of opinions." This definition indicates that a conference must be a two-way communication. In other words, each person participating in the conference must have an opportunity "to contribute" as well as "to receive" messages. In this respect, a good conference is much like a good conversation in which there is free flow of dialogue among all of the participants. A conference is not a occasion when one person "lectures" to another person. In fact, any conference which is dominated by one of the participants is not, by definition, a "conference" at all.

The Need for Conferences.

In the absence of good communication between a student teacher and his supervisor, learning to teach becomes very much a matter of

115

chance. Admittedly, one can learn by stumbling upon good teaching techniques and by making mistakes. However, the student teacher who has the ready help of a perceptive supervisor will learn much better by capitalizing on the experience and insights of this supervisor.

Sometimes it is tempting, in view of a supervisor's busy schedule, to rely on impromptu "catch as catch can" conferences with student teachers. It is also sometimes tempting for a supervisor to hold a conference only "when one is needed." While both of these procedures are understandable and even have some merit, they can lead to the potentially dangerous situation in which there is a communication gap between the supervisor and the student teacher. To guard against this situation and to provide the student teacher with an optimal learning situation it is essential that the supervisor hold regularly scheduled conferences with the student teacher. While the frequency of such conferences will vary from situation to situation, it is probably desirable to hold a minimum of one regularly scheduled conference each week. These regularly scheduled conferences will insure that the student teacher and supervising teacher have opportunities to share ideas and generally communicate with one another. Often times, during such conferences, problems are gradually uncovered that would otherwise go undiscovered, undiscussed and unsolved.

WHO SHOULD CONFERENCE?

Since there are a number of different people involved in a typical student teaching situation, there is a need for conferences between different sets of people to establish and maintain the necessary communication network for a successful student teaching experience. For instance, there is a need for conferences between the student teacher and supervising teacher, between the student teacher and principal, between the student teacher and college supervisor, between the supervising teacher and college supervisor, and between the college supervisor and principal. Furthermore, there is a need for three-way conferencing among the student teacher, supervising teacher, and college supervisor. Likewise,

Problem Situation: 22

The supervising teacher asks the college supervisor how to get her new student teacher to open up and talk more during conferencing. What advice do you have for her?

there may be a need for three-way conferences among the student teacher, supervising teacher, and principal. While all of these conferences between people will have a great deal in common, each has its unique aspects. The uniqueness and special problems concerning conferences between different people will be briefly explored in the following section.

Student Teacher and Supervising Teacher.

Conferences between the student teacher and supervising teacher are the most common and most important of all. In many aspects, conferences between these two people are also the easiest to arrange and conduct. This is so because the student teacher and supervising teacher are together much of the time and have an opportunity to get to know one another quite well. However, as has been pointed out elsewhere in this chapter, supervisors sometimes erroneously assume that since they spend so much time with the student teacher there is no need to hold regularly scheduled conferences. Of course, the potential problem of not setting aside time for periodic conferences is the danger of not finding the time to discover and deal with the more subtle problems that do not surface during the typical, hectic, regular school day.

Student Teacher and College Supervisor.

The role of the college supervisor varies considerably from college to college thus making it difficult to generalize about conferencing problems between the student teacher and college supervisor. For instance, many colleges and universities are changing the role of the college supervisor in such a way that he spends less of his time observing student teachers and more of his time training supervising teachers and helping with the in-service training program of the cooperating school district. In such instances, the cooperating teacher assumes more responsibility for direct supervision of the student teacher. When this is the case, the college supervisor typically has less need or time for conferences with individual student teachers. However, in the more traditional role of the college supervisor where he spends much of his time observing individual student teachers, there is considerable need for conferences between the student teacher and college supervisor.

One of the unique problems inherent in conferences between the student teacher and college supervisor is that the college supervisor often represents a "threat" to the student teacher. This comes about partly because the college supervisor does not work day-in and day-out with the student teacher and therefore has less opportunity to establish rapport than does, for instance, the supervising teacher. Then too, the student teacher realizes that the college supervisor has a larger voice in determining the student teacher's grade. All of this means that the college supervisor must make a conscious effort to establish rapport and open up lines of communication with the student teacher. And of course, regularly scheduled conferences provide an excellent opportunity for the college supervisor and student teacher to know and trust one another.

Problem Situation: 23

A student teacher tells you, the principal, he has received conflicting directions from the supervising teacher and the college supervisor. What suggestions would you offer the student teacher?

Student Teacher and Principal.

Ideally, a principal should find the time to get to know each student teacher in his building. In fact, a principal should observe and take the time to hold at least one conference with each student teacher.

A principal can contribute much to the student teaching experience. For instance, a student teacher should learn about the administrative problems of the cooperating school. Due to his unique position in the school, the principal can provide the student teacher with insights into many educational problems. The conference provides a vehicle by which the principal can make these contributions to the student teacher. The principal must overcome the same basic problems as the college supervisor—namely, establish rapport and trust—if he is to conduct effective conferences with the student teacher. The principal typically is not able to spend a lot of time with each student teacher. Most principals maintain an "open door" policy whereby they encourage faculty members to drop in and visit at any time. Such a policy would be a good one for student teachers also. The principal must realize, however, that many student teachers would be too timid to do so. Therefore, it is advisable for the principal to take the initiative to arrange at least one regularly scheduled conference with each student teacher to insure at least a minimum of communication.

Supervising Teacher and College Supervisor.

Just as the supervising teacher must establish communication with a student teacher so must he communicate effectively with the college supervisor. This is often a difficult task because the college supervisor usually is not able to visit the school very often. Furthermore, when the college supervisor does visit, he often has a busy schedule trying to see many people. Then too, the supervising teacher's schedule typically permits little free time for conferencing with the college supervisor. In addition to these problems, both the supervising teacher and college supervisor are often somewhat anxious about their relationship with one another. Then too, the supervising teacher might view the college supervisor as a visiting expert who may disapprove of some of the things happening in the supervising teacher's classroom. On the other hand, the college supervisor is often anxious about being welcomed as an outsider in the student teaching triad. Many of the anxieties can be alleviated if time is found for the supervising teacher and college supervisor to conference periodically. Such conferencing will provide an opportunity to discuss the student teacher's progress and minimize the danger of misunderstandings arising between the cooperating teacher and college supervisor.

College Supervisor and Principal.

The college supervisor should confer with the principal each time he calls on the school. This will provide an opportunity to talk about any aspect of the student teaching experience that may be desirable. It will also enable the principal and college supervisor to develop an understanding of one another's expectations regarding student teachers and other teacher trainees in general.

Student Teacher, Cooperating Teacher and College Supervisor.

Just as conferences between two parties involved in the student teaching experience are important, so is it essential that conferences among three or more of these parties be held periodically. Perhaps the most obvious need for such group conferences is the three-way conference between the student teacher, cooperating teacher, and college supervisor. This trio of key people in the student teaching experience must be constantly in communication with one another. Three-way conferences provide an excellent opportunity for them to do so. Ideally, such a three-way conference should be held as a part of each college supervisor's visit. Of course, as previously mentioned, time does not always permit such extensive conferencing. At the very least, however, a conference among these three individuals should be held at the mid-point and at the end of the student teaching experience. The mid-term conference is important because it provides an opportunity to check all facets of the student teaching experience while there is still time to make changes. This mid-term conference provides an opportunity to take stock of the student teacher's progress up to that point and to help the student teacher work on any weaknesses that may be evident at that point. Also, the mid-term conferences provide an opportunity to discuss the learning experiences the student teacher has had during the first part of the student teaching period and make plans for rounding out his experiences during the time remaining.

A three-way conference near the end of the student teaching period can also serve many important functions. For instance, it provides an opportunity to discuss the final evaluation of the student teacher. It also allows the supervising teacher and college supervisor to help the student teacher reflect on and draw conclusions from the student teaching experiences. Such a reflection can help the student teacher develop greater insights into teaching, explore employment potentials, and examine graduate study needs.

While it is impossible to specify the exact number of three-way conferences which should be held among the student teacher, the supervising teacher and college supervisor, nevertheless it is essential that these three people communicate adequately to insure a successful student teaching experience.

Sometimes it is useful to have four and even five-way conferences among the people involved in student teaching. For instance, a conference among the student teacher, supervising teacher, college supervisor and principal can serve many useful purposes. Also, it is often useful to arrange a group conference among several student teachers and the college supervisor. Of course, in the final analysis, each supervisor must decide how many and what types of conferences are necessary in any given student teaching situation.

TYPES OF CONFERENCES

Continuous.

A very effective form of conferencing is that which is carried on continuously and informally as the student teacher and supervisor work side by side throughout the student teaching experience. This is especially true in the case of elementary student teachers who typically spend a good deal of time with their supervising teachers. It is usually more difficult for secondary student teachers and their supervisors to find time for continuous informal conferencing due to the nature of the typical high school schedule.

Impromptu conferences, such as these, have a number of advantages.

For one thing, they provide a vehicle for dealing with problems as they arise. If a problem must wait until the next regularly scheduled conference, it is often forgotten, or at least loses its immediacy and the "teachable moment" is lost. Continuous conferencing also provides an excellent opportunity for a student teacher and his supervisor to break down barriers, get to know each other and generally develop the kind of rapport that is essential for working together to create a successful student teaching experience. Yet another advantage of continuous conferencing is that it provides sufficient time for the unhurried exploration of a wide range of topics associated with teaching. Lastly, continuous conferencing can provide the relaxed informality that facilitates effective communication. Student teachers are more likely to reveal their genuine concerns and problems in the friendly, non-threatening atmosphere of an informal conference.

Scheduled.

While continuous conferencing has many advantages and is perhaps the single most valuable approach to conferences, the regularly scheduled conference is indispensable in the student teaching experience. The greatest value of the regularly scheduled conference is that it guarantees a periodic block of time when the student teacher and his supervisor can isolate themselves, and undistracted by other problems, really communicate about the student teaching experience. As was pointed out earlier in this chapter, due to the extremely busy and often hectic schedule of both the student teacher and his supervisor, it can be difficult to find the amount of time to confer that is required if the student teacher is to have an optimal learning experience. The regularly scheduled conference helps to insure that the supervisor and student teacher will have some blocks of time set aside to communicate with one another.

Many supervisors find it advantageous to hold at least one scheduled conference each week. Of course, some student teachers need more frequent conferences than others and therefore each supervisor must decide how often conferences are necessary.

DEVELOPING CONFERENCE SKILLS

Conducting effective conferences requires a good deal of skill. For most supervisors it will require much dedication and effort to develop and refine these skills. Following are some of the common skills necessary to conduct effective conferences.

Listening.

Since a conference involves "receiving" as well as "contributing," a supervisor must develop the ability to really listen to the student teacher. Perhaps the first step toward becoming an effective listener is to develop the will to listen. One must really want to hear to be an effective listener.

Is it possible for a supervisor to improve his listening skills. However, this is a difficult task because listening is largely an attitudinal skill. If one wishes to listen, he will probably listen well. On the other hand, if one is not really interested in listening to someone, in all likelihood the listening will be superficial. So an excellent way to begin improving one's listening skills is to cultivate an attitude of really wanting to listen closely to a student teacher.

Providing Positive Reinforcement.

The typical student teacher is somewhat anxious and insecure and therefore in need of positive reinforcement. Reinforcement involves complimenting or praising the student teacher for the things he does well. The use of reinforcement is predicated upon the notion that "success breeds success." Reinforced behavior tends to be repeated and it is obviously desirable that a student teacher repeat the things that he already does well.

There are a variety of ways that a supervisor can provide reinforcement for a student teacher. One of these simply involves telling the student teacher verbally, in some straight-forward manner, that he has done a particular thing well. Another way to reinforce a student teacher is with non-verbal cues such as a pleasant smile, an approving nod of the head, or any of the other non-verbal behaviors that are interpreted as approval.

The subject of reinforcement is dealt with in some detail in Chapter Eight which deals with behavior modification with student teachers. Behavior modification is very much dependent upon the utilization of positive reinforcement techniques. Suffice it to repeat at this point that the effective supervisor must develop and refine reinforcement skills if he wishes to conduct successful conferences.

Offering Constructive Criticism.

Yet another conferencing skill that is essential for a supervisor to possess is that dealing with offering constructive criticism to the student teacher. The supervisor must develop a fair degree of rapport with the student teacher before offering very much constructive criticism. In the absence of good rapport, even mild constructive criticism can be very threatening to most student teachers. However, if the supervisor has been able to establish a trusting relationship with the student teacher, he can then offer constructive criticism without destroying the student teacher's confidence.

Of course, constructive criticism must always be offered in a tactful manner. Fortunately, most supervisors realize the importance of avoiding caustic and degrading criticism. Such criticism is not only antagonizing and demanding but also destroys the student teacher's confidence. Each supervisor must develop the ability to tactfully offer constructive criticism to student teachers in a non-threatening way if he is to conduct effective conferences.

Another suggestion that can improve conferences is the recommendation that supervisors avoid offering too many constructive criticisms at any one time. Likewise, a student teacher who is given a dozen suggestions for improvement is likely to become bewildered and not know which areas to concentrate on improving.

Problem Situation #24

A student teacher, who is having rather severe discipline problems, asks your advice. What suggestions would you give him?

Developing an Improvement Plan.

Each conference should end with something specific that the student teacher can do to improve his performance as a teacher. This improvement plan should be developed cooperatively by the supervisor and the student teacher. It has already been pointed out that an improvement plan should concentrate on one or two areas. A supervisor might ask the student teacher what the one or two things might be upon which she would like to concentrate. Or, a supervisor may wish to be more direct and simply suggest to the student teacher an area that she should strive to improve. It is perhaps less important that a supervisor use a specific technique for developing an improvement plan than it is to get such a plan developed and secure the student teacher's committment to it.

The supervisor should not only help the student teacher decide which areas need improving, but also help her decide on a strategy for bringing about this improvement. Such strategies, of course, will vary from student teacher to student teacher. A supervisor should follow-up, perhaps at the next conference, to make sure that the student teacher has in fact made an effort to improve in that particular area.

The important point concerning improvement plans and their systematic development and assessment is that more often than not student teachers do not improve their teaching performance by chance, but rather by a conscious organized attempt to improve.

Use of Audio or Video Feedback.

The development of audio and video tape recording equipment has provided the supervisor with a new set of tools that is useful in working with student teachers. For instance, as previously mentioned, a supervisor can audio or video tape a student teacher in action, and then structure a conference around the play-back of this audio or video tape. A student teacher who has an opportunity to hear and/or see himself in action is likely to gain insight into his strengths and weaknesses through this experience. A perceptive and skillful supervisor can help the student teacher analyze the audio or video tape. Of course, a video tape provides more complete feedback than does an audio tape. So whenever possible, it is recommended that a video tape recording be used in preference to an audio recording. However, if a video tape recorder is not available, all schools now have audio tape recorders which can easily be used to record a lesson that a student teacher is teaching.

Video tape packages are now available which are quite portable. While not all schools yet have such taping equipment, where such equipment is available it is recommended that student teachers be given the benefit of this valuable learning experience. To do this, simply set the television camera up in the back of the classroom and let it run during the lesson. It is not necessary to obtain broadcast quality picture or sound. Then allow the student teacher to see the playback of the video tape several times, stopping it whenever desirable to discuss some facet of the lesson. A supervisor might even wish to keep the video tape and compare it with later tapes so that the student teacher can check on his progress during the student teaching assignment.

The conferencing skills that have been discussed in this section, (listening, providing positive reinforcement, offering constructive criticism, developing an improvement plan, and utilizing audio or video feedback) will help enable the supervisor to provide the student teacher with a rich environment for learning. In a real way, this should be the ultimate goal that the supervisor has for each conference held with a student teacher—to provide a rich environment for learning.

SUMMARY

In summary, each student teaching supervisor must develop the ability to conduct effective conferences with student teachers. As this chapter has pointed out, there are different types of conferences and a variety of skills that a supervisor must refine to communicate effectively with the student teacher. Just as there is no single best way to teach, likewise there is no single best way for a supervisor to conduct conferences. Conferencing techniques that work well for one supervisor may not work well for another. Likewise, conferencing techniques that are effective with one student teacher may not be effective with another. Therefore, it behooves each supervisor to develop a wide variety of conferencing skills and strategies so that any particular technique can be skillfully employed at the appropriate moment. Also, and perhaps even more difficult, the supervisor must be able to decide which supervisory skill or strategy is most appropriate in each conferencing situation. The ability to do so characterizes the truly professional conferencer.

CHAPTER EIGHT

The Use of Behavior Modification in Teacher Education

> The story is told about the Missouri farmer who was beating his mule over the head with a piece of two by four. A teacher (who also supervised student teachers) happened by and asked the farmer why he didn't use reason, patience, and kindness with the animal rather than force. To which the farmer replied, "I do, but ya got to get his attention first."

At times, those of us who work with student teachers seem to be guided by this Missouri farmer's philosophy. We intend to use reason, patience and kindness with our student teachers but feel that first we should be tough on them.

This chaper explores an alternative to the "get tough" philosophy of student teaching supervision.

What is Behavior Modification?

Behavior modification is a relatively new development in teacher education. "Behavior mod," as it is often called, involves the use of a variety of planned and conscious techniques to modify or change human behavior. When applied to pre-service teacher education it represents an attempt to improve the teaching behavior of a teacher education student. Behavior mod techniques may be useful at many points throughout the teacher education program.

The Nature of Behavior.

It is important, in any discussion of behavior modification, to realize that all human behavior is learned. This is true, whether the behavior is good or bad. It therefore seems logical that, since all behavior is learned, one should be able to change behavior by using learning principles. Behavior mod is built upon this assumption.

Problem Situation: #25

Mary is doing her student teaching in a sixth grade and is engaged to be married. Her supervising teacher tells the college supervisor that Mary is doing an excellent job in her student teaching; however, recently she has been seen necking with her boyfriend in his car in front of the school before school starts in the morning. If you were the college supervisor, what would you recommend to the supervising teacher?

Understanding why people in general or student teachers specifically behave as they do is a difficult task. For instance, few supervisors ever totally understand why a student teacher has trouble controlling students in a class where there is poor discipline. Likewise, it is difficult to understand why a student teacher is defensive about constructive criticism, or has trouble getting along with other teachers, or is resistent to a change that seems logical and necessary to the supervisor.

Behavior modification is also built on the assumption that a supervisor has the ability to objectively analyze and understand a student teacher's behavior. If a supervisor cannot do so, he will probably have difficulty employing behavior modification techniques with student teachers.

Praise Versus Criticism.

There are many techniques that can be used to change human behavior and each of these techniques is based on a slightly different philosophy. These different techniques can be placed on several continuums. For instance, Figure 7:1 shows a continuum which has "praise" at one extreme, and "criticism" at the other extreme.

This figure is intended to illustrate that a supervisor could, for example, using nothing but positive reinforcement (praise) in an attempt to bring about desirable changes in a student teacher's behavior. In other words, a supervisor at this extreme end of the continuum would attempt to reinforce all desirable behavior that the student teacher might exhibit. Conversely, the supervisor would ignore all undesirable behavior that the student teacher might exhibit in hopes that this behavior would

Figure 7:1 Criticism-Praise Continuum

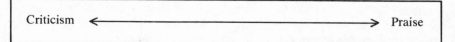

Criticism ⟵—————————————⟶ Praise

be extinguished. On the other hand, a supervisor could, if he wished, use only criticism with a student teacher—a position represented by the extreme left end of the continuum shown in Figure 7:1. Such strategy would be, in the opinion of these writers, ill-advised; however, it does represent an extreme option and helps to illustrate the praise versus criticism concept.

Nondirective Versus Directive Supervision.

Figure 7:2 shows yet another continuum which helps explain different approaches to behavior modification. This continuum shows that a supervisor, at one extreme, can be totally nondirective in dealing with a student teacher. At the other extreme in Figure 7:2 a supervisor can

Figure 7:2 Nondirective/Directive Continuum

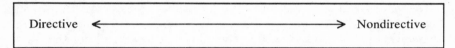

be totally directive. A nondirective supervisor would capitalize on whatever the student teacher is interested in—his problems, successes, questions, concerns, anxieties, joys, aspirations, etc. The directive supervisor in less concerned with the student teacher's interests and more concerned with telling, giving directions, and generally guiding the student teacher with a rather firm hand. The nondirective supervisor spends a good deal of the time "listening" while the directive supervisor spends more time "talking" to the student teacher.

As one might expect, the philosophy represented by nondirective supervision is very different than that represented by directive supervision. For instance, the implication behind nondirective supervision is that a person will work hardest to improve those things that he feels should be improved. If a supervisor subscribes to this philosophy, he will be primarily concerned with what the student teacher believes to be his weakest area. Although the supervisor may disagree with the student teacher's perception, the nondirective supervisor will pursue the felt needs of the student teacher. Nondirective supervision also is predicated on the belief that sooner or later a student teacher will discover the weaknesses by himself that a directive supervisor might have pointed out in the first place. Another important point in the philosophy behind nondirective supervision is that most student teachers are more receptive to nondirective supervision. As might be expected from messages contained throughout this book, the authors believe that nondirective supervision is best with most student teachers.

By way of contrast, the philosophy behind directive supervision suggests that the typical student teacher needs a good deal of direction and if left to himself, would not discover his own weaknesses. While it is probably true that some student teachers would in fact benefit from directive supervision, it is also true that the vast majority of student teachers will, with relatively little help from the supervisor, discover their own strengths as well as weaknesses.

One of the potential problems of a highly directive approach to supervision, is that it is likely to cause the student teacher to become rather dependent upon the supervisor. If a supervisor feels that it is important for student teachers to develop the ability to self-evaluate themselves so that after entering the profession they can continue to improve their teaching skills through self-evaluation, then a supervisor will likely utilize directive techniques sparingly.

The praise/criticism and directive/nondirective extremes shown in Figures 7:1 and 7:2 are probably rarely appropriate for utilization in the supervision of student teachers. Rather, most supervisors find that techniques suggested by the middle of these continuums are more appropriate for use with student teachers.

REINFORCEMENT

Problem Situation: #26

Mrs. Kay, a twenty-eight year old student teacher in a kindergarten, comes to the Director of Student Teaching because she is anxious about how well she is doing in her student teaching. She likes her supervising teacher and college supervisor but is worried about doing a good job and anxious about the kind of recommendation she will get. What thoughts would go through your mind if you were the Director of Student Teaching?

Types of Reinforcement.

There is a wide variety of reinforcement techniques available for use. For instance, when behavior mod is used with young school children, reinforcement such as toys, tokens, money, or even food have been successfully used to get the learner to repeat desirable behavior. These same tangible reinforcers have been used successfully with abnormal children.

Of course, student teachers are normal mature individuals, and therefore, the appropriate reinforcers for them differ considerably from those employed with younger or abnormal individuals. Student teachers are likely to find reinforcers such as approval and a favorable letter of evaluation rewarding. Perhaps the ultimate reinforcer is that which has been called "a sense of mastery" wherein a learner is reinforced by the acquisition of new knowledge or skills simply for the "sake of learning."

It has been speculated that not all reinforcers will work equally well for all learners. A supervisor must recognize that one student teacher will be reinforced by one thing—perhaps a smile of approval on the part of the supervisor—while another student teacher will receive reinforcement from a glowing written evaluation.

Types of reinforcement can also be conveniently divided into verbal and non-verbal categories. A supervisor may tell a student teacher verbally that she did a particular thing very well. On the other hand, a supervisor may, through non-verbal cues such as an approving nod of the head or a pleasant smile, communicate to a student teacher approval of a job well done without actually saying a word.

Selecting Proper Reinforcers.

Once a supervisor has developed the ability to utilize a variety of different types a reinforcers, he must also develop the ability to select the appropriate reinforcer for a given student teacher in a given situation. A supervisor will have to experiment with different reinforcers to find those that are most appropriate for each student teacher. He will likely discover that a particular student teacher seems to react best to certain reinforcement techniques. Of course, the supervisor should continue utilizing those reinforcers which seem most successful with each student teacher.

The supervisor who is able to establish rapport quickly with a student teacher will have an advantage when it comes to selecting appropriate reinforcers to use with that student teacher. Establishing rapport is discussed in greater detail elsewhere in this book, however, it is mentioned here in passing as an important condition for helping the supervisor understand a student teacher well enough to select appropriate reinforcers.

Setting Up a Reinforcement Schedule.

Once a supervisor has developed competency in utilizing different reinforcers, and has discovered which reinforcers seem to work best

Supervising teachers need to select the appropriate reinforcers for a given student teacher in a given situation.

with a given student teacher, he is then in a position to set up a reinforcement schedule for a student teacher. A reinforcement schedule is simply a plan for systematically providing reinforcement for a student teacher. Some student teachers will need a reinforcement schedule that calls for the liberal use of reinforcers whenever he does something well. Other student teachers may require a reinforcement schedule that calls for the use of relatively few reinforcers. By the same token, some student teachers will require a longer continuous use of reinforcement than others.

A reinforcement schedule should be constructed so as to eventually lead the student teacher to exhibit the desired behavior without the need of external reinforcers. In other words, the supervisor should gradually withdraw the reinforcement that he provides and help the student teacher shift to internal reinforcers. Put into other words, the goal of the supervisor should be to help the student teacher become self-motivated to exhibit the desired behavior.

A supervisor will need to experiment with establishing reinforcement schedules for student teachers. And of course, reinforcement schedules should be modified as time goes by in accordance with what a student teacher seems to require.

Evaluating the Outcome of Reinforcement.

A supervisor must constantly evaluate the success of the reinforcement efforts that he makes with each student teacher. Reinforcement techniques must be changed as a student teacher matures. A supervisor must be perceptive enough to realize when a particular reinforcement technique is not working with a student teacher. This is difficult to do, because the results of reinforcement are subtle and difficult to detect. It is only over a period of time that a supervisor can hope to see tangible improvement in a student teacher as a result of the reinforcement that had been applied.

THE "WELL DONES" APPROACH TO BEHAVIOR MODIFICATION

One new approach to helping a student teacher modify his behavior is that called the "Well Dones Method."* It emphasizes the positive—the student teacher's strengths or "well dones." This behavior mod technique consists of the following components.

Before the Conference.

The supervisor asks the student teacher to jot down, over a period of a week, his well-dones (W/D's)—the things he does well in the classroom. Also, the supervisor asks the student teacher to record his opportunities for improvement (O/I's) as he notices them. The student teacher is also asked to write an example for each W/D and O/I listed. Before each conference, the supervisor observes the student teaching (for no less than 50 minutes), and notes a number of major W/D's and one or two O/I's. The supervisor also identifies supporting examples for each W/D and O/I observed during his stay in the classroom.

Discussing the Well-Dones.

The student teacher comes to the conference with the W/D's and O/I's in writing; the supervisor brings his W/D's and O/I's. The conference begins with a discussion of the student teacher's W/D's so that the instructor identifies and continues to build upon his strengths. This allows the interview to begin positively. Wherever appropriate, the supervisor asks the student teacher to "say a little more," to "give

*The Well-Dones approach to supervision was developed by Dr. Daniel Kralik at Northern Illinois University. The authors wish to thank Dr. Kralik for the material presented in this section.

an example," to "talk about the W/D's" which he listed. During the discussion regarding the W/D's the supervisor adds or supports the W/D's with those he noted during his classroom observation, or he adds his W/D's when the student teacher completes discussing his W/D's.

Notes may be jotted down by either the student teacher or the supervisor during the interview. If the supervisor does the writing she should check with the student teacher to be sure that what is written is agreeable to him.

Discussing the Opportunities for Improvement.

After the W/D's are discussed, the supervisor shifts the discussion to the O/I's by saying something like: "Let's go to the O/I's now." The supervisor may suggest O/I's to the student teacher but should do so cautiously. This is especially true if this is the first conference with the student teacher. After the student teacher has discussed his O/I's, the supervisor asks him to identify "one major O/I which he would most like to work on."

Problem Situation: #27

A junior high school science teacher is having trouble deciding whether or not to leave his student teacher alone in the class. The student teacher is rather nervous and unsure of herself in front of the class. He asks your advice as the college supervisor. What would your advice be?

Developing Courses of Action.

Taking the one major O/I upon which the student teacher would most like to work, a specific course of action is written which includes: who, does what, by when. The course of action is developed by the supervisor asking the student teacher what he would like to do which would be helpful to change the O/I. If the student teacher is unsure about what to do, the supervisor can offer specific suggestions, which should include possible alternative courses of action. After several possible courses of action are discussed, the supervisor asks what specific action the student teacher plans to take. His reply is written alongside the appropriate O/I and includes the specifics; i.e., John, video tapes a classroom session, by November 1st.

Closing the Conference.

It is suggested that the supervisor close the conference by asking if there are additional ways he can be helpful to the student teacher. He might even ask the student teacher for one major well-done and one major opportunity for improvement regarding his work as a supervisor. Not only does this help the supervisor identify changes which he should be considering, but it helps demonstrate that evaluation is a two-way process. Another alternative is to ask for feed-back regarding what the student teacher thought of the conference and the way it was conducted so that the supervisor can continue improving his conferencing skills.

Follow Through.

Following the conference the supervisor writes down the major O/I and the course(s) of action which was determined in the form of a memo. A copy of the memo is given to the student teacher and the supervisor keeps a copy so that he can talk with the student teacher at appropriate checkpoints to see how things are going, and to offer additional help. The memo also helps the supervisor more clearly understand the changes which the student teacher is undertaking. The supervisor is also therefore more able to offer support and reinforcement to the student teacher.

Questions About the Well Dones Approach.

Several questions often arise regarding the use of the Well-Dones Method. Some frequently asked questions are: With which student teacher is it least likely to be effective? How does the supervisor suggest O/I's which he observed in the classroom? Do many student teachers analyze themselves in a rather superficial or "safe" way using the Well-Dones Method? What qualities must the supervisor possess to make the Well-Dones an effective tool? With which student teacher is it likely to be effective? It has been found that most student teachers are receptive to the Well-Dones Method (90% or more). There seem to be three kinds of student teachers who are resistant to its use: (1) the student teacher who questions his own effectiveness or senses that you question his effectiveness, (2) the student teacher who interprets any kind of evaluation to be a violation of his rights, and (3) the student teacher who resists any kind of change. Once these student teachers are identified it is suggested that more traditional approach be used with them. One should limit the use of the Well-Dones Method to those student teachers who are receptive, and use an alternative form of supervision with others. The Well-Dones program is aimed at helping our many effective student teachers to become even better.

How does the supervisor suggest O/I's which he observed in the classroom? Some supervisors are very concerned about getting their "two cents in." It is suggested that supervisors be cautious about pressuring the student teacher to accept the supervisor's point of view. The supervisor should concentrate his efforts on causing student teachers to change in a direction which is desirable to the student teacher, rather than attempting to force change. During the discussion of the O/I's, the supervisor may mention an O/I which he observed in the classroom (including specific examples from his classroom observation), but the student teacher should decide which major O/I he wishes to work on. An exception to this is the rare student teacher whose performance is marginal and who may be failed, but for these few student teachers the Well-Dones Method is probably less appropriate.

Do many student teachers analyze themselves in a superficial or "safe way" using the Well-Dones Method? Few student teachers do this. Most student teachers are receptive to improving themselves and they realize that their self-analysis is a major element of the Well-Dones program. A superficial analysis results in a waste of the student teacher's time and does little to improve the professional and personal relationship between the student teacher and supervisor. However, it may be necessary for a shy or insecure student teacher to test the Well-Dones Method by writing less threatening W/D's and O/I's for the first Well-Dones conference. If the student teacher develops confidence in the supervisor's abilities and intentions during the initial interview, he may analyze himself in greater depth during the second Well-Dones conference. Supervisors should be aware that it may take some time to reduce such fears, and working on a minor area could lead to developing the trust essential for tackling a major problem in the future.

What qualities must the supervisor possess to make the Well-Dones an effective tool? In the hands of a skillful supervisor, the Well-Dones program can be a very effective tool for improving teaching effectiveness. Some essential qualities for the supervisor to possess if the Well-Dones approach is to be used are: (1) the desire to help student teachers improve rather than forcing them to change, (2) a people-oriented versus an autocratically oriented philosophy, (3) creativeness and resourcefulness sufficient to help suggest workable solutions to problems, and (4) the ability to be a good listener; that is, the ability to restate the thought and feeling tone of the student teacher's idea.

Rather than assuming that the supervisor possesses the above qualities it might be enlightening for the supervisor to ask for student teacher feedback regarding each of the above four qualities.

SUMMARY

In conclusion, behavior modification has a great deal of potential use with students engaged in clinical experiences. It is up to every supervisor to decide which behavior modification technique is most appropriate with each student teacher. Just as there is no one best way to teach, likewise, there is no one best behavior modification technique. The supervisor should be aware of the various modification techniques that are available for use, should be able to skillfully use a variety of these techniques and perhaps most important and difficult of all, must be able to decide which technique is most appropriate to use in a given situation with a given student teacher.

CHAPTER NINE

Evaluation

Problem Situation #28

The Student: I worked harder than my roommate and she received an "A" in student teaching and I only received a "B."

The Classroom Supervisor: A "B" is a good grade—no student teacher is perfect and an "A" to me, means perfection. When I student taught I only received a "B" and I worked plenty hard.

The College Supervisor: I know there is a better way to evaluate students in student teaching. I wish the Dean would buy the credit-no-credit proposal.

The Problem

Of particular difficulty to the individual responsible for the supervision of the various clinical experiences is the act of evaluating. Most classroom teachers enjoy working with prospective teachers in a clinical environment but when the time arrives for final evaluation it frequently has a traumatic effect. If one surveyed those responsible for the classroom supervision of student teachers, and rated what they disliked about supervision the most—the task of evaluating would win handily. Some teacher education institutions have tried to protect the classroom teacher from this undesirable task by making the college supervisor responsible for the student teachers' evaluation. In the strictest sense, this is only proper as the college is ultimately legally responsible for the administration of the program and the grading of students. To be realistic however, the classroom teacher who daily interacts with the student involved in clinical experiences is the only logical one to really evaluate. Unfortunately, or fortunately, depending on one's perspective, the college supervisor is just not in the environment enough to adequately evaluate the student.

Problem Situation #29

Supervising Teacher: What, another evaluation form? I was just getting used to the one your college developed last year.

College Supervisor: Oh, this one is much better. It's based upon performance objectives.

Supervising Teacher: Performance what?

The College Role

The college has a very important role in the evaluation of a student involved in clinical experiences. One of the major reasons for the trauma of evaluation on the part of the supervising teacher is the fact that colleges have not been much help.

There are many ways the colleges can ease the uncertainty of evaluation and make the task more palatable. Materials pertaining to the evaluation of clinical experiences should be distributed and discussed with prospective classroom supervisors prior to the arrival of the student. During conferences, building or grade level meetings, seminars, or formal classes, the goals, objectives and techniques of evaluating the student should be carefully discussed to better enable the supervising teacher to understand and perform his important role.

In addition to college developed evaluative materials it should be kept in mind that the most effective materials are those which are developed cooperatively. When developing clinical experience objectives, explanatory materials and evaluation forms, input from the classroom supervisors should be obtained during the developmental process. By doing this, many of the concerns, problems, and questions which the supervising teacher may have during the evaluation process may be accommodated.

The college supervisor is of particular importance in providing understanding and support to the supervising teacher in the evaluation procedure. As mentioned in previous chapters, the college supervisor should be available to lend support to the supervising teacher. Nowhere is that support needed more than in the area of evaluation. All materials used during the evaluation procedure should be discussed with the classroom supervisor prior to their use. The purpose and use of the various evaluation instruments should be carefully explained. The grading system should be interpreted. Various techniques utilized in evaluation should be discussed and above all, emphasis should be placed upon the fact that evaluation should be both formal and informal and that the informal method should be continuous. Supervising teachers must realize that college students enrolled in clinical experiences have a tremendous desire to know how well or how poorly they are doing. Because of this, supervising teachers should periodically hold both formal and informal conferences with the student to discuss progress. It is interesting to note that after the clinical experience is concluded—most students feel that they did not have enough discussion concerning evaluation. If tutorial, observational, participatory, student teaching, or internship experiences are to be meaningful; students, upon completion, must be able to understand their strengths and weaknesses. How else will they grow into the type of classroom teacher the profession needs? The importance of continuous evaluation cannot be over-emphasized.

Although the supervising teacher must be the main evaluator because of daily interaction with the student involved in clinical experiences, the college supervisor must still be an integral part of the evaluation process. As previously mentioned, the college representative must provide the supervising teacher with materials concerning evaluation, and interpret the evaluation procedure, the philosophy, objectives, and importance of evaluation. Above all, however, he must observe the student involved in clinical experiences enough so that if a supervising teacher wishes to discuss a particular student, the college supervisor has a basis for discussion. In addition, the college student is the direct responsibility of the college supervisor and must at all times be protected from unjust evaluations, personality conflicts, or lackadaisical attitude on the part of the supervising teacher. Evaluation is a cooperative process and although the classroom supervisor is the prime evaluator, the college supervisor needs to be greatly involved and be prepared to participate.

The college can also be a facilitator of the evaluation process and greatly ease the burden placed upon the supervising teacher by removing letter grades as a part of the evaluation. The use of letter grades in clinical experiences is poor practice. Letter grades have added to the trauma of evaluation by placing on an outside agency (the classroom supervisor) the obligation of assigning letter grades. This situation has perpetuated strained relationships between the student teacher and supervising teacher and even between the college supervisor and the supervising teacher. In addition most supervising teachers are reluctant to give poor grades resulting in an extremely high percentage of "A's" and "B's."[1] Because of the emphasis upon letter grades, emphasis on the evaluation itself tends to center around the grade. Students are extremely grade conscious and rather than being concerned with the development of strengths—they become concerned with "how to obtain an A." Interpreting the grading system to the supervising teacher is also extremely difficult because to many supervising teachers, involved in a K-12 grading system, a "C" is an average grade. Relatively few "C" grades are given at the college level and therefore is regarded by hiring officials as quite inferior.

[1] Various studies proved that at Central Michigan University during the period when letter grades were given—approximately 95% received "A" or "B."

Colleges should take a hard look at the grading system utilized in clinical experiences and encourage changing from a letter grade to a system of pass-fail or credit-no credit. A 1969 study indicates that supervising teachers prefer not giving grades, student teachers overwhelmingly prefer a credit-no credit system, and school administrators felt the credit-no credit system to be quite satisfactory.[2]

Johnson, in his study entitled "A National Survey of Student Teaching Programs"[3] reported that 82% of the institutions nationwide which had student teaching programs reported use of the letter grade system for evaluating student teaching experiences. In Michigan, Meyer and Quick found that 85% of the institutions in 1968 continued to use a letter grade system in evaluating student teachers but approximately 85% of the students enrolled in student teaching programs received a credit or no credit evaluation. This data would indicate that although Johnson's information regarding the percentage of institutions using letter grades for student teaching is accurate, the number of students actually affected by such a policy is far less. It would appear that the larger state teacher education institutions in Michigan generally utilize a credit-no credit type of student teaching evaluation while the smaller, private institutions in the state, in 1968, still used the letter grade system.

Moving to a credit-no credit method of evaluation tends to focus upon the real objective of a clinical experience; the process of becoming a teacher and it tends to relieve some of the anxiety that supervising teachers have concerning evaluation.

THE STUDENT TEACHER IS A PART OF THE EVALUATION PROCESS

Problem Situation #30

Principal: John is the best student teacher we have ever had in the building.

College Supervisor: What do you mean?

Principal: He didn't send one student out of his room to my office and his study halls were always quiet.

---

[2] Meyer, John and Quick, Alan F., "Let's Do Away With Letter Grades in Student Teaching," *Supervisor's Quarterly*, Volume 6, Number 1, Autumn, 1970.

[3] James A. Johnson, *A National Survey of Student Teaching Programs*, multi-state Teacher Education Project, Monograph II, 1968, pp. 43.

Evaluation is Important to the Learner

John might have been a very mediocre student teacher but he had heard from fellow students that in order to get a good student teaching evaluation—the principal must be impressed and John knew what impressed most principals. John was, then, directly involved in the evaluation. Maybe he was a little too involved—but involved.

The evaluation of any clinical experience is especially important to the student. The experience provides an opportunity to translate knowledge gained in a college classroom to the real world of teaching and the resulting evaluation will have a great effect upon whether or not the student will get the position he desires. By and large, students are highly motivated and do a very competent job, yet student teaching must be regarded as a learning experience. Therefore, it behooves the supervising teacher and college supervisor to constantly provide the feedback necessary to provide a learning environment. This should be done both informally and formally and on a daily, weekly, midsemester and final evaluation basis. Not only should it be done on a continuous basis, but the evaluation process should also involve as many professionals as possible. For instance, if a student teacher works with more than one supervising teacher—both should evaluate the experience the student had under each. If the student teacher has spent time coaching debate, dramatics, athletics, or assisted the band or orchestra leader, or participated in any co-curricular activity—the responsible supervisor should complete an appropriate evaluation form. There are evident reasons for this. One very good reason is to enable the learner to ascertain strengths and weaknesses. Secondly, hiring officials state that the most important documents in one's placement credentials are the evaluations concerning the clinical experience. It is only logical that the more supporting evidence a candidate can supply concerning performance in a clinical experience—the more the chances for employment are enhanced. In addition, the more evaluations tend to indicate a variety of experiences the greater the appeal to hiring officials.

The evaluation of clinical experiences is, therefore, extremely important to the student for two reasons. One—it is a learning device and aids the learner to determine progress so that he can improve upon weaknesses and be cognizant of strengths, and in addition, it provides the prospective teacher's credentials with an important document. Because of the latter importance, it behooves the supervising teacher and college supervisor to ensure that very careful consideration be given the final evaluation. In this competitive teacher market, an honest, carefully written analysis of the clinical experience can be a prime factor in the student obtaining a position.

It is especially important and beneficial for the learner to objectively evaluate himself. Self-evaluation has proven to be an excellent technique. Many supervising teachers use the method of having a student list his strengths and weaknesses. This list forms the basis for a discussion concerning evaluation of progress. Another effective method of self-evaluation is to have the student and supervising teacher complete identical evaluation forms for discussion purposes. Regardless of the technique used in self-evaluation, the fact is that for sound evaluation to take place—the student must be involved. He must understand the criteria being used, he must receive constant feedback concerning progress, and he must be involved in assessing his own progress and ability. Above all, supervising teachers must remember that evaluation is not secretive but rather an open dialogue. The student should see and discuss his final evaluation prior to it being submitted to the college. One way to insure that this happens is for the student to sign his name to the form indicating that he has had the opportunity to read the document but that he does not necessarily agree with its content. This method at least indicates that the student has had the opportunity to read the final evaluation and hopefully discuss it thereby utilizing the evaluation as a learning device rather than merely a routine chore.

TOOLS TO AID THE CLASSROOM SUPERVISOR IN THE EVALUATION PROCESS

Problem Situation #31

Student Teacher: She may have said it—but I didn't hear her.

Supervising Teacher: I said it, but he must not have listened.

Good Communication.

By now, it is assumed the reader realizes the importance of the evaluation of clinical experiences. It is not enough, however, to only realize the importance. The college supervisor and classroom supervisor must utilize various techniques to ensure that proper communication between the supervisor and the learner takes place. Proper communication is always a skillful process and communication concerning how well one is performing takes a special skill. Most students are sensitive to criticism and supervisors need to be aware of this. Any discussion concerning progress should be carefully thought out. Timing and choice of words are extremely important. Positive communication is directly related to positive rapport between the supervising teacher and student. If an open, friendly, helpful environment has been created for the student by the supervisor, the chances for positive communication between the teacher and the learner are greatly enhanced. If the supervising teacher works at developing a positive relationship, the chances for good communication concerning evaluation are greatly improved.

There are numerous techniques which supervising teachers can use in evaluating students. One of the most popular is to perform the lesson critique. The student has planned a lesson, discussed its objectives with the supervisor and teaches it. The supervisor then critiques the lesson utilizing observation, an audio tape recorder, or a video tape recorder. Discussion is then held as soon after the presentation as possible. This method has many positive attributes for it provides immediate feedback when a situation is fresh in both the student and supervisor's mind.

The advantage of an arrangement such as that shown in Figure 9-1

Figure 9:1: A Typical Physical Arrangement for Video Taping a Student Teacher

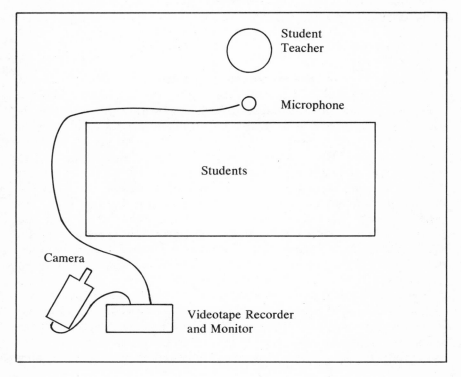

Student Teacher

Microphone

Students

Camera

Videotape Recorder and Monitor

is that it can be set up and taken down in approximately five minutes, and the only equipment in the front of the classroom is the lavalier microphone around the student teacher's neck. By using a zoom lens, it is possible to obtain both wide angle and close-up shots with the camera, placed in the back of the classroom as shown in Figure 9-1.

Critiquing using observational techniques does not entail a great deal of expertise but the evaluation should be based upon:

(1) The stated objectives
(2) The utilization of appropriate teaching techniques
(3) The results of a particular lesson—based upon learner performance

Audio Tape Recorder

The use of an audio tape recorder depicts voice projection and other good speech techniques as well as accuracy, conciseness, and thoroughness of the material taught. The audio tape recorder which is extremely easy to use, is especially effective in evaluating presentation of material and appropriateness of voice.

Video Tape Recorder

In recent years the use of video-tape recorders to assess the student teaching experience has become increasingly popular. More and more college supervisors are seen prowling the halls of various school buildings with a video-tape back pack. These machines are relatively lightweights and can easily be transported from building to building. It is hoped that not only will college supervisors use the VTR's, but that supervising teachers will. Supervising teachers can usually obtain a video-tape recorder on loan from the college supervisor or obtain one from the district instructional materials center. Not only are video-tape recorders often available from these sources but the authors have noted the prevelancy of building housed video-tape recorders. These modern VTR's are relatively easy to learn to operate and an informal session between the college supervisor and the interested supervising teachers will often suffice.

Using the video-tape for evaluation purposes, however, is another matter. Supervising teachers must apply evaluation and assessment criteria to the video-tape recorder. A seminar presented by the college supervisor could well be devoted to the analysis of teaching effectiveness as viewed via the VTR. The purpose of using the VTR in student teaching evaluation is to provide feedback to the student concerning the effectiveness of presenting a lesson. The supervisor, in assessing this, may wish to develop a VTR evaluation sheet or use one of the several evaluation forms already in use at various teacher education institutions. One such form is the Indiana University-South Bend self-evaluation check sheet. This sheet designed for use by a student viewing his own presentation via the VTR could well be used by both the supervising teacher and student to establish a joint discussion concerning the lesson presentation. [4]

One will notice that Yutzy refers to the Flanders Interaction Analysis System in his evaluation scale. There are various types of descriptive category systems which supervising teachers and college supervisors may use as a tool for collecting specific, objective type data about teacher and pupil reaction to teachers in classroom settings and which might be adapted to a self-derived evaluation form. These various methods of studying the teaching styles help greatly to analyze specific aspects of the teaching situations and lend an opportunity for analytical conferences between the student and supervisor concerning techniques of teaching. The use of the interaction analysis designs has proven especially helpful in helping student teachers plan, execute and analyze their own teaching behaviors.

Furst states in the Association of Teacher Education *Research Bulletin #10* entitled "Interaction Analysis" that "One of the exciting commonalities in the results cited is that, in all cases, there were some significant differences in either attitudes or behaviors of students trained in interaction analysis when they were compared with students not so trained." [5]

INTERACTION ANALYSIS SYSTEMS WHICH HAVE EVALUATION IMPLICATIONS

The Flanders System

The above mentioned Flanders system of Interaction Analysis is likely the best known and most widely used classroom observation system in existence. One of the real advantages of this system is that supervising

[4] James A. Yutzy—"Self Evaluation and Videotaping Toward High Quality Teaching and Vision," a monograph, presented at ATE Clinic, DeKalb, Illinois, May, 1973.

[5] Sandefur, J. T. and Bress ler, Alex A. "Classroom Observation Systems In Preparing School Personnel" *Interaction Analysis Selected Papers, Bulletin #10, 1971.* Much of the material in the section of this chapter concerning observational styles has been taken from this excellent source. The authors suggest this source for those individuals desiring to learn more about these systems.

Figure 9:2: Video Self Evaluation Check List

1.   Aesthetic (Cosmetic) Characteristics

	pleasant		unpleasant
Voice	I	I	I

	appropriate		inappropriate
Appearance	I	I	I

2.   Interaction Characteristics (a la Flanders)

Teacher

	much/many	some	little/none
Accepts feeling	I	I	I
Praises	I	I	I
Utilizes student ideas	I	I	I
Questions	I	I	I
Lecture	I	I	I
Directions	I	I	I
Corrects	I	I	I

Pupil

Responses to teacher	I	I	I
Responses to other students	I	I	I

3.   Evaluation of Competencies
a. Did I achieve my purposes/objectives? _____
   Does the objective possess a situation, a behavioral term and
   an acceptance level statement? _____
b. Type of questions asked: Illustrate, write in
   Cognitive memory _____
   Convergent ___ _____
   Divergent _____
   Evaluative _____
c. Creativity: cite illustrations
   Creative incidents
   Open-ended, divergent thinking
d. Human Interaction skills (statements)
   Impact of my behavior on others
   Association of my internal and external self
   Differential treatment in the classroom

Empathetic listening and responding
Concreteness and specificity of communication
e. Non-verbal communication (Body language, facial
   expressions, use of eyes, hand)
   What do I need to change, to practice, and to improve?

teachers and college supervisors can learn and adopt the system in a short period of time. The Flanders system has ten categories: seven are for teacher verbal behavior, two are for pupil talk, and one is to denote silence or noise.

The Flanders system has ten categories. The seven listed above represent teacher verbal behavior.

Indirect influence encourages student participation in classroom discussion. When a teacher asks a question, a student is invited to form his own ideas and express his own opinions or facts. When the teacher uses a student's ideas or accepts an answer and praises him, he encourages the pupil to participate freely.

Direct influence has the tendency to inhibit student initiative and promote compliance. The restriction of student freedom through direct teacher influence—lecturing, criticizing, justifying authority, or giving

Figure 9:3: Flanders Verbal Behaviors

The teacher-verbal categories are divided into two groups. Four are considered to exert indirect influence on the classroom atmosphere and three to exert direct influence. In addition there are three categories concerning student talk.

Indirect Influence Categories
 1. Accepts pupil feeling
 2. Praises or encourages pupil
 3. Accepts or uses pupil's ideas
 4. Asks questions

Direct Influence Categories
 5. Lectures
 6. Gives directions
 7. Criticizes or justified authority

Student Talk Categories
 8. Student talk-response
 9. Student talk-initiation
10. Silence or confusion

direction—results in less student freedom to act. Direct teacher influence is provided for in category No. 8, which is student response to the teacher. This category depicts a narrow response to a specific question. Category 10 is for silence, short pauses, and moments of confusion that often occur in classroom interaction.[6]

In the Flanders Interaction Analysis system, the observer uses a coding system to report the category occurring during a specific period of classroom interaction. In this way, the supervising teacher or college supervisor, acting as an observer, may use the results of the observation to discuss teaching style and classroom climate with the student teacher. This system is popular with many college supervisors and supervising teachers. It adds structure and method to observations and studies indicate that the Flanders system and others have contributed to a student teacher's understanding of his teaching style.

OTHERS SYSTEMS WHICH MAY BE HELPFUL

Other systems which may be used effectively for classroom observation are:

1. *The Verbal Interaction Category System (VICS)*—developed by Edmund Amidon and Elizabeth Hunter. The approach expanded the Flanders system to provide more detailed information. The system is used when the verbal communication of teachers and students is being observed.

The system contains five major categories for analyzing classroom verual behavior: teacher initiated talk, teacher response, pupil response, pupil-initiated talk and other. Similar to the Flanders system, the various categories of verbal behavior must be learned in order for the observer to analyze and code teaching styles.

2. *Assessment of Quality of Teaching in Elementary Schools*—Marie Hughes. This is affectively (concerned with the emotional climate in the classroom) oriented and is both a verbal and nonverbal record of communication. It has been used effectively to train student observers in elementary school classrooms. Hughes developed a comprehensive set of categories in which to classify teacher behavior. The seven major categories are:
   A. Functions that control
   B. Functions of imposition of a teacher

[6] Ibid.—Interaction Analysis—ATE Bulletin #10

C. Functions that facilitate
D. Functions that serve as personal response
E. Functions of positive affectivity
F. Functions that develop content by response
G. Functions of negative affectivity

3. *The Arno Bellack system* is an analysis into the linguistic behavior of the teacher and learner and is therefore classified as cognitive. (Those observational systems which are concerned primarily with intellectual activities.) It is primarily concerned with the kinds of meanings that are transmitted between teachers and learners. Tape recordings and transcripts are used for data collection.

   The speaker is recorded and coded, depending upon whether teacher or pupil. The code reveals whether the speaker is structuring (focusing attention on a topic), soliciting, responding to a solicitation, or reacting to a response. The Bellack system of coding further identifies substantiative meaning—what the student or teacher is talking about—and the substantiative logical process or defining, stating facts, explaining, justifying, etc.

   The purpose of the system is to determine how much the teacher or student talks. Bellack hopes that through this type of observational system that a classroom climate will be developed and perpetuated in which the teacher is not the most active class member and classroom climate is developed whereby students initiate questions and react to them.

4. *Milton O. Meux and Othanel B. Smith and their collaborators,* in 1959, began a study to consider the logical aspects of teaching behavior and to determine a logical structure for teaching subject matter. The major purpose of this study was to develop a means of dividing verbal behaviors of the student and teacher into units to be analyzed. This cognitive approach is the beginning step towards development of a theory of classroom instruction with a basis of a logical analysis of behavior.

5. *Spaulding Teacher Activity Rating Schedule (STARS)*—Robert L. Spaulding. This approach is designed to view teachers as they try to bring about changes in pupil behavior. The system is designed for observation in cognitive, social, or motor. Spaulding found out that three types of teacher variables were linked with pupil performance and self-concept. They were:
   a. Supportive, approving, and receptive pupil behaviors which operated as rewards.
   b. Adverse or dominative teacher behaviors which had generally a punishing effect, and

c. Limit and goal setting teacher behaviors which tend to qualify, regularize, organize, or further structure and environment for the benefit of pupil performance.

These findings were based upon a study that involved 113 categories of teacher pupil transactions in twenty-one elementary classrooms. According to Sandefur and Bressler, this system requires an extensive period of time to train observers (two and three weeks) which may make this system prohibitive to most supervising teachers and college supervisors.

6. *Multidimensional Analysis of Classroom Interaction (MACI)*— Fred K. Honigman. This system is based upon categories for coding and quantifying the classroom behaviors of teachers and students and is based upon the Flanders System.

   MACI contains two categories dealing with a teacher's reactions to and use of pupil's feelings. In addition, a category is included which provides the observer with a code to use when students talk with a level of feeling. There is a category for student hostility and the system also focuses on the teacher's means of involving students in the classroom and allows for determining whether students participate by being called upon or whether they volunteer to talk.

   Honigman suggests that a 20 to 30 minute observational period be used.

7. *Observation Schedule and Record (OScAR)* Donald M. Medley and Harold E. Mitzel.

   Primarily the instrument developed by Medley and Mitzel is a means to quantitatively record data concerning teacher behavior.

   OScAR5U, the latest revision of the instrument is an 18 category schedule that has been designed to be used in direct observation of the behavior of teachers while they teach and while their students learn. The category system has an affective, cognitive, and procedural dimension which shows the amount of time the teachers and students spend on matters other than classroom content.

   The primary value of the system is that it provides a language of teacher behavior and it provides a specific feedback concerning just how the teacher performed. It can show many teachers the behaviors and patterns of behavior that they use daily in the classroom. The OScAR System may be used by observers after limited amounts of training.

It is fair to say that observational systems while really not new on the teacher evaluation scene, are not in widespread use. Most likely there are many reasons for this and some may be:

1. Many educators still regard teaching as an art and not a science. The observation systems mentioned are looked upon by many as scientific and therefore are often rejected.

2. Teacher Education institution personnel are generally poorly versed in these systems, and, therefore, are not in a position to provide help to supervising teachers.

3. Classroom observational systems have received their greatest acclaim in the affective domain and, unfortunately, many educators are still concerned primarily with the cognitive domain.

Observational systems have an important role to play in aiding the supervising teacher and college supervisor to more objectively evaluate the prospective teacher.

INFORMAL EVALUATION

It is hoped that the point has been made in the preceding pages, that an important obligation of the supervising teacher and college supervisor is to evaluate. Whether a system for evaluation is used or whether the evaluation is semi-structured using a system developed by the college or individual supervising teacher—evaluations need to be made and are the basis for feedback to the student involved in clinical experiences.

The question is often asked by the supervising teacher or college supervisor—"How often shall I evaluate?" There is no right or wrong answer that can be given to this. A common sense answer would be—enough to provide feedback so that the clinical experience is a learning situation and so that the mid-semester and/or final evaluation will be accurate, comprehensive, and point out strengths and weaknesses which should contribute to the student's becoming a successful teacher.

One of the most important and successful techniques of evaluating students involved in clinical experiences is the informal evaluation. Informal evaluation is a period, long or short, during the school day, when the supervisor has the opportunity to discuss the progress of the student. This is not a situation whereby the supervisor says, "Well, it's time for evaluation, let's talk," but rather an informal period whereby the supervisor provides feedback as to what was effective or not so effective during a particular lesson or day. Because working with a student in a clinical experience should be people-oriented—that is, the supervisor has to effective at working with people, it is important to always begin an evaluation situation whether it be formal or informal, with positive comments. No matter how poor a student may appear—there must be something positive that an evaluator can convey. It would be the greatest of exceptions when this is not possible. In addition, evaluation should always be based upon some established criteria. If it is a structured observation, talk to the points in the system. If it is based upon the college evaluation criteria—use the evaluation form provided by the college. One of the real problems for students when evaluated is that the supervisor will come out with a critical comment about a characteristic about which the student has had no forewarning. One rule in working effectively with a student in a clinical experience or any student for that matter, is to lay ground rules at the outset of the experience. If the supervisor has expectations of the student—let the student know of these—early. Remember, communication, to use the cliche, is a "two way street." Informal evaluation is a time to assess the student's progress. It should be performed as often as possible and will make formal evaluation much easier. A supervisor must remember that evaluation should be continuous and feedback positive, constructive and immediate.

FORMAL EVALUATION

Evaluation is Important to the Student Teacher

All institutions of higher education require some form of mid-semester, mid-term, or final evaluation of student teaching experiences. Some use the open letter of recommendation by the supervisor to serve this purpose; others have developed rather sophisticated and often complicated forms. Some colleges require these to be done in multiple copies and most require that they be typewritten. In some instances, the supervising teacher is the sole evaluator, in others only the college supervisor, while still others use both and even include the building administrator. Regardless of who completes the final evaluation of the experience there are some key points that should be remembered. One, that the evaluation will serve as a reporting device to the student concerning progress and teaching potential and to the School or Department of Education for the issuance of credit and recommendation for certification. Secondly, that the final recommendation form will also be included in the student's credentials, if so desired, for future employment purposes. Based upon these assumptions, the key points for a supervisor to take into consideration when completing final evaluation forms are:

1. The form should be accurately and neatly typewritten. A supervisor must remember that the form represents the student in the eyes of the employer. A messy, haphazard form will undoubtedly have adverse effects upon the hiring official. In addition, the form represents you, the supervisor.
2. The grade level and/or subjects taught should be clearly stated.
3. The type of school setting should be mentioned. Such situations as traditional, non-graded, team teaching, non-ability grouped, modular scheduling, open classroom, etc. have special importance to the hiring official.
4. The type of area such as urban, inner city, suburban, rural as well as economic status of area is oftentimes relevant information for hiring officials.
5. The type of building—elementary, middle or junior high or senior high as well as building enrollment should be mentioned.
6. The amount of responsibility the student enrolled in the field experience had is important. Such items as number of classes taught, activities performed, etc. should be included.
7. Judgments concerning performance and potential should be made on specified criteria. Criteria often used in field experiences are:

Personal Qualities

   a. Self-Concept: The student accepts and uses criticism, is poised and self-confident, practices constructive self-evaluation.
   b. Sense of Humor: The student has ability to laugh at himself, he encourages wit but not sarcasm; he sees the appropriateness of humor in teaching.
   c. Appearance: Grooming and attire are appropriate to school standards.
   d. Health: The student displays stamina, alertness and energetic behavior; there is an absence of chronic illness. He displays positive and optimistic attitudes; he is seldom upset; he is emotionally stable.
   e. Industry: The student is dependable; he accepts and carries out responsibilities; he displays ambition and enthusiasm.

f. Reliability: The student is punctual; his attendance is acceptable in light of the circumstances.

Human Relations

a. Rapport with students: The student relates well with all pupils and is able to develop mutual respect; he shows genuine liking for pupils.
b. Rapport with Staff: he relates comfortably with peers, staff and administration; he is cooperative and follows policies and procedures appropriate to the respective roles that exist within the school.
c. Rapport with others: The student relates well with parents and other community residents; he uses tact and diplomacy in dealing with such other persons.

Communication Skills

a. Oral: The student's voice is clear and pleasant as evidenced by varied inflection, good modulation and rate; he is effective in giving clear directions and interesting presentation; he practices good grammatical skills and speaks without serious impairment; his language is appropriate to grade level.
b. Written: Written material is accurate in spelling, grammatically correct, clear and concise in meaning, legible and appropriate to grade level.
c. Graphic: The student supplements oral and written communication with visual reinforcements such as illustrations, examples, charts, audio-visual, etc.

Academic Preparation

a. General Knowledge: The student is well read and knowledgeable as evidenced by his interest in and ability to converse on a wide range of subjects.
b. Subject matter: The student displays an in-depth knowledge and understanding of his teaching field as shown by his ease in discussion and using content in organizing instructional materials; he utilizes contemporary application of subject material; he is competent in locating necessary and appropriate instructional materials.

Classroom Effectiveness

a. Planning and Organization: The student consistently uses and implements both long and short range planning; he incorporates the use of behavioral objectives reflecting the ability and needs of pupils; he involves pupils in planning; he is flexible in using plans, being willing and able to deviate; the timing and sequence of activities reflect a concern for the use of classtime.

b. Methods and materials: They are appropriately selected for the attainment of planned objectives; they are relevant to pupil levels and current societal needs. The student uses and accepts pupil ideas in classroom interaction; he utilizes a variety of methods and materials.

c. Evaluation: The student uses oral, written and pupil self-evaluation for measuring the achievement of stated objectives; he is fair and consistent in pupil evaluation; he uses evaluative data for planning future learning activities and as positive assessment of pupil needs; he uses multiple sources of data for determining pupil needs; he maintains accurate documentation of evaluative data.

d. Motivation: The student considers the individual needs of pupils in selecting learning activities and materials; he effectively uses clear illustrations, practical applications, challenging question and problems; he establishes high expectancy levels with all learners; he applies basic principles of learning theory.

Professionalism

a. The student knows and behaves in compliance with the teacher code of ethics; he participates in professional meetings, demonstrates interest in professional growth; he is alert to the need for school policies as evidenced by his ability to accurately interpret school policies to others; he is knowledgeable regarding the organization, structure, and function of professional associations and of the school as a social institution.

8. A well written, in depth, narrative should accompany an evaluation. This narrative should be structured to expand upon each of the above mentioned criteria. For example under the criteria "Personal Qualities:, one might say:

"George has a good personality for teaching. He is sure of himself with pupils and enjoys their spontaneity and humor. Though not especially witty, he sees the place of humor in the classroom. George's health is excellent—he is energetic and alert. His good mental health is evidenced through poise, calmness, and self-confidence. He is always anxious to be critiqued but was not as adept at self-evaluation. This improved after video-taping. George was very dependable and reliable and worked hard at his teaching. His clothing was less conservative than typical for the community, but was not disconcerting."[7]

9. The student being evaluated should have the opportunity to read and discuss it with the evaluator. Yes—even the final evaluation or recommendation that goes into his placement files.

10. The University supervisor should always discuss the final evaluation with the supervising teacher.

11. The student teacher, college supervisor, and supervising teacher should sign the evaluation.

12. The evaluation should be dated.

13. The university supervisor should submit a comment for placement purposes for every student under his guidance. These comments also should always be discussed with the student involved.

14. All evaluation forms concerning students should be turned into the college supervisor just prior or concurrently with the conclusion of the student teaching experience. It is too easy to procrastinate completing the evaluation once the student has left the environment. Remember, the earlier these are sent to the university supervisor, the greater the opportunity for the student to obtain a position.

Final evaluation is so very important to all involved that special care must be devoted to ensure that a meaningful, honest, comprehensive report be submitted. After all, students enrolled in student teaching experiences do not get reimbursed. The final evaluation is, in reality, their reimbursement for the time and effort they have devoted in this important experience.

[7] Central Michigan University Student Teaching Evaluation Form, Revised, 1973.

SHOULD PUPILS PARTICIPATE?

Pupils Should be Given Evaluation Guidelines

One aspect of evaluation yet to be covered is the area of pupil evaluation. The evaluations of students involved in clinical experiences by pupils under their guidance can be meaningful and greatly contribute to the understanding of one's performance if the evaluation is structured in a serious vein. Pupils as early as the fourth grade can contribute to the evaluation of a clinical experience student provided they are given certain guidelines. The authors advocate pupil evaluations and would recommend:

1. That the evaluations be relatively unstructured and that open ended questions be used. Such as:
   a. What did you like about the class?
   b. Was the teacher fair?
   c. Did the teacher care for you?
   d. What didn't you like about the class?
   e. What suggestions would you make to help the teacher?

The advantage of these types of open-ended questions is that students

With proper guidelines, pupils can evaluate student teachers.

are able to express themselves in their own words and are often candid and honest.

2. That the evaluations be anonymous.
3. That the evaluations be discussed with the supervising teacher and college supervisor.
4. That the student realize that by and large, pupils enjoy college· students and tend to be generous in their evaluations.
5. That supervising teachers and college supervisors respect the evaluation of pupils but that their own evaluations are based upon established criteria and not biased totally by pupil opinions.

Used appropriately, pupil evaluations can be of real service to the student teacher. Care, however, should be taken in the interpretation of the comments.

SUMMARY

The evaluation of a student involved in a clinical experience has caused great difficulty in the past. Students have charged that the evaluations have not been frequent or effectively communicated. Supervising teachers have often resented having to be the "keeper of the gates," well realizing that a poor evaluation could prevent an· individual from certification and employment. Colleges, realizing the problem, have spent a great deal of time and effort toward pre-service and in-service work with supervising teachers concerning evaluation as well as developing helpful materials. A movement toward collaborated evaluations between college and K-12 personnel is evident and many larger teacher education institutions are using credit-no credit as a basis for evaluation. All of these factors have contributed to more frequent and more comprehensive evaluations.

CHAPTER TEN

The Future of Clinical Experiences in Teacher Education

My warmest congratulations go out to each of you for the decision you have made to follow a teaching career.

Today—as never before—we rest our hopes for America on the teachers of America. We know that our future is being forged in the classrooms and campuses of our nation. We see the wisdom of an uncompromising commitment to educational excellence and expansion.

So you have chosen well. And America will be richer for your dedication to a task that holds the promise of a better tomorrow.

I wish you Godspeed as our nation's custodians of opportunity for the children who will inherit the precious heritage we share.

Lyndon B. Johnson

There are a number of current trends in American teacher education which hold potential implications for the future of clinical experiences in teacher education programs throughout the United States. A number of these trends will be discussed in this chapter.

Increasing the Clinical Component in Teacher Education.

The first of these trends involves increasing the amount of clinical experiences in pre-service teacher education. For one thing, the length of student teaching is being increased at many colleges and universities. Many colleges now require a full semester of student teaching. It is also becoming common along with the increased length of the student teaching assignment to provide multiple placements, each in a different setting, for the student teacher. For example, an elementary student teacher might have two different placements, each at a different grade level. A history student teacher might student teach in a junior high school and then in the senior high school.

Clinical experiences are also being initiated at an earlier period in many teacher education programs. Clinical experiences starting in the freshman or sophomore year are becoming increasingly common. These early clinical experiences might include observation, participation, teacher aiding, tutoring, community agency work—a wide variety of different kinds of experiences with youth. This means that in the future clinical experiences are going to occupy an even more important position in teacher education than they now do. This also means that supervising teachers are destined to play an increasingly important role in teacher education.

This increased emphasis on the clinical component of teacher education is reflected in the National Council for the Accreditation of Teacher Education (NCATE) standards. These standards state:

1.3.3 *Teaching and Learning Theory with Laboratory and Clinical Experience.* As distinguished from the Content for the Teaching Specialty and the Humanistic and Behavioral Studies, there is a body of knowledge about teaching and learning that should be the basis for effective performance. If teaching is to be more than a craft, teachers need to understand the theoretical principles which explain what they do. For this reason, the study of teaching and learning theory is included as part of the professional studies component. However, like the study of other empirical theory, the study of teaching and learning theory requires laboratory experiences through which the student may conceptualize principles and interpret their application to practical problems. Much of what has been called "general methods" and "special methods" can therefore be taught as the application of teaching and learning theory.

Whereas the study of teaching and learning theory provides the prospective teacher with principles of practice, and the laboratory exercises illuminate and demonstrate these principles, clinical experience confronts the student with individual cases or problems, the diagnosis and solution of which involve the application of principles and theory. Certain kinds of problems (such as planning, selection of learning difficulties, individualization of instruction, classroom management, and evaluation) represent recurring types of classroom situations. Clinical teaching involves the student in the diagnosis and "treatment" of the individual problem, under the guidance of an experienced teacher. Because it is now possible to simulate many of these situations or to display a selection of real problems electronically, and because the prospective teacher's efforts can be recorded, viewed, and reviewed—it is now feasible to give much effective clinical experience outside the school classroom.

Standard: *The professional studies component of each curriculum includes the systematic study of teaching and learning theory with appropriate laboratory and clinical experience.*

1.3.3a In what courses, seminars, and readings are provisions made for the study of teaching and learning theory?

1.3.3b What practices or procedures show that the study of teaching and learning theory requires and is accompanied by laboratory experiences (observation, demonstration, problem-solving, tutoring, microteaching, and/or other direct experimental activities)?

1.3.3c What are the provisions for clinical experience (diagnosing and treating individual typical cases, practices, or problems)?

1.3.3d What information shows that the instruction in the study of teaching and learning theory incorporates the findings of research and other scholarly writings; and provides experiences for students in their interpretation and use?

1.3.3e What data indicate that all prospective teachers have laboratory and clinical experiences under the guidance of an experienced teacher?

1.3.3f What evidence shows that the programs of study for all prospective teachers include the systematic study of teaching and learning theory with appropriate laboratory and clinical experience?

1.3.4 *Practicum.* "Practicum" refers to a period of experience in professional practice during which the student tests and reconstructs the theory which he has evolved and during which he further develops his own teaching style. It provides an opportunity for the student to assume major responsibility for the full range of teaching duties in a real school situation under the guidance of qualified personnel from the institution and from the cooperating elementary or secondary school. It presupposes the learning experiences included in all other professional studies; it is not a substitute for them. It is a more complete and concrete learning activity than laboratory and clinical experience.

It is assumed that the institution carefully selects the cooperating schools used for practicum and that it establishes effective working arrangements with these schools.

Practicum in most situations may be called student teaching; in some situations it may be called a type of internship.

Standard: *The professional studies component of each curriculum for prospective teachers includes direct substantial participation in teaching over an extended period of time under the supervision of qualified personnel from the institution and the cooperating school.*

1.3.4a What evidence shows that every prospective teacher assumes substantial responsibility over an extended period of time for the range of teaching duties in the professional role for which he is being prepared?

1.3.4b What information shows that relationships between professional personnel in the institution and in the cooperating schools contribute positively to students' experience in practicum?

1.3.4c What evidence confirms that the supervision of students in practicum is organized. and executed under the direction of qualified personnel from the institution?

1.3.4d What information shows that the supervising teachers in the cooperating schools are superior teachers, are trained in supervision, and are committed to the task of educating teachers?

1.3.4e What systematic methods are used to record or describe the teaching performance of students and how is the resulting data used by students and supervisors to analyze teaching behavior?

1.3.4f How is the supervision of students in practicum translated into an index of faculty load? For how many students in practicum does each teacher education faculty member have responsibility?

Problem Situation:

> If you were asked to devise an ideal teacher education program what would your recommendations be?

Greater Reliance on Elementary and Secondary School Personnel.

Another trend in teacher education is for colleges and universities to rely more and more on elementary and secondary school personnel to help plan, supervise, and evaluate clinical experiences. At its best, this trend could dramatically improve teacher education. At its worst, it could lead to a mere "dumping" of teacher education students on the already overburdened public schools. It will take careful planning and diligent effort by both the public schools and colleges to insure the first and prevent the latter from happening.

In any event, this trend makes is imperative that public school and college personnel join hands in planning and executing higher quality clinical experiences. Much of this book has represented an effort to provide guidelines that will be helpful to public school and college personnel as they undertake this exciting task.

Competency Based Teacher Education.

Yet another trend in teacher education which holds great potential implications for the supervision of student teachers is the trend toward competency-based teacher education (CBTE) or performance-based teacher education (PBTE) as it is sometimes called. Competency-based teacher education involves an emphasis upon the "competencies" that a teacher must possess to be a successful educator. In other words, a competency-based teacher education program would start by carefully determining the competencies and skills that a teacher should possess as well as determination of what would constitute observable evidence of such competencies. The next step toward a teacher education program based on competency would be the developing of a series of learning experiences that would help the future teacher acquire and refine the necessary competencies. More often than not such a teacher education curricula would be highly individualized wherein each student could work at his own pace through a series of learning modules designed to help the student acquire the necessary competencies. Also, in a typical competency-based teacher education program there is a heavy reliance on early and extensive clinical experiences designed to help the future teacher develop the necessary competencies. It is through a series of clinical experiences that the future teacher is able to demonstrate that he has indeed acquired the competencies.

The implications of the competency-based teacher education movement for supervisors of clinical experiences are many. For one thing, it will be imperative that supervisors understand the concepts behind the competency movement. It will also be essential that the supervisor be familiar with the various competencies that the particular college or university has established for its teacher education program. Furthermore, it is necessary that a supervisor have the skills to evaluate how successfully a student teacher is in fact demonstrating each particular competency. This may mean that a supervising teacher will have to develop new evaluation skills. Of course, the supervisor should possess these same competencies that the student teacher is expected to acquire and demonstrate. Yet another characteristic of a CBTE program is that the objectives of the program along with the requisite competencies must be made explicit and public. In other words, a student going through a competency-based teacher education or the faculty members teaching in such a program (including supervisors of clinical experiences) must clearly understand and accept the objectives and competencies associated with the program. Furthermore, the student is held accountable for ultimately exhibiting the required competencies. So another implication of competency-based teacher education programs is that all student teaching supervisors (including those in the public schools) must clearly understand the objectives of the competencies associated with the program so that they in turn can not only help the student practice and refine the competencies, but also hold them accountable for these competencies.

So, to the degree that competency-based teacher education becomes widely adopted in teacher education, it may well be that future student teaching supervisors will have to become much more intimately involved with college-based teacher educators in helping to devise the list of required competencies and in executing the CBTE program.

Problem Situation: #33

If you were asked to list the ten most important competencies for a student teaching supervisor to possess, what would you list?

Competency-Based Student Teaching Supervision.

Just as it is appropriate for a future teacher to develop certain essential teaching competencies, it is also appropriate for a student teaching supervisor to develop certain "supervision" competencies. Therefore, as one might expect, concurrent with the CBTE movement is a trend toward competency-based student teaching supervision. A number of experiments dealing with competency-based student teaching supervision are currently being conducted throughout the United States. While this movement is in an early and relatively crude stage of development, it is likely that a trend toward competency-based supervision will grow from these early efforts. In the meantime, it behooves all student teaching supervisors to seriously consider the question of what skills or competencies are required to successfully supervise student teachers. Having answered this question—it behooves supervisors to practice, develop and refine those supervision competencies so that he may employ them in working with student teachers.

Field-Centered Teacher Education.

Yet another move in teacher education which has implications for student teaching supervisors is the movement toward "Field-Centered" teacher education programs. Field-Centered teacher education programs may be defined as those which offer all or nearly all of the professional educational components of teacher education out in the field (in an elementary or secondary school). A typical field-centered teacher education program is structured around a teacher education center which is cooperatively developed and operated by a public school system and a college or a consortium of some type. In such a program, the elementary and secondary school teachers become full partners with college faculty members in designing and delivering the teacher education component. One of the advantages of a field-centered teacher education program is that the future teachers are provided a ready laboratory in which to develop and refine teaching skills. It is relatively easy to combine theory and practice in a teacher education program that is field-centered. There are many models of field-centered teacher education programs now functioning in the United States. However, in all of these programs, the student teaching supervisor takes on an increasingly important role. As with the other new directions in teacher education mentioned in this chapter, the field-centered teacher education program relies more heavily on elementary and secondary teachers than do the traditional teacher education education programs.

Increased Use Of Media.

It has already been pointed out in previous chapters that many colleges are now using television and other media in their student teaching programs. As television equipment becomes more refined, portable, and economic, and as teacher educators have more opportunity to experiment with its use, this and other forms of media will undoubtedly be used more and more in teacher education.

Simulation.

A number of colleges are now experimenting with the use of "simulation" in their teacher education programs. Simulation is a technique developed for the training of pilots during World War II which has since found application in a wide variety of fields. Teacher educators have found the simulation technique useful in helping train teachers because it provides the education student with a "life-like" teaching problem to which he must respond as a teacher. Depending upon the sophistication of the simulation program being used, it is even possible to feed back simulated responses to each student response, much in the same way that teaching machines utilize branched programs. This learning device is certain to be increasingly utilized in future teacher education programs.

Internships.

Internships became popular during the teacher shortage era as a means of providing teacher training to liberal arts graduates. As the teacher shortage ended, the nature of internships changed. This new form of internship typically involves anywhere from a half year to a full year partially paid teaching assignment. These interns are typically supervised by a college supervisor as well as a supervising teacher from the local elementary or secondary school in which the intern is placed. Often interns have a class of their own and are supervised more like a first year teacher than like a student teacher. However, some internships are in reality very much like a regular student teaching assignment.

While the nature of internships vary considerably from institution to institution and not all institutions utilize the internship concept; nevertheless, it appears that a new form of internship will likely grow in popularity in teacher education in the future.

SUPERVISION BY OBJECTIVES

Yet another movement in teacher education which seems destined to grow in the future is that centered around the "supervision by objectives" concept. As the phrase implies, supervision by objectives represents an attempt to help supervisors devise and be guided by objectives that have been clearly thought through and written down. This procedure for clinical supervision is based on the earlier work of Cogan[1] and more recent works of both McNeil[2] and Goldhammer.[3] Supervision by Objectives[4] also provides for the systematic participation

[1] Cogan, Morris. *Supervision at the Harvard-Newton Summer School*, Harvard Graduate School of Education, 1961. (Mimeographed)

[2] Goldhammer, Robert. *Clinical Supervision.* Holt, Rinehart and Winston, Inc., 1969.

[3] McNeil, John D. *Toward Accountable Teachers: Their Appraisal and Improvement.* Holt, Rinehard and Winston, Inc., 1971.

[4] The "Supervision by Objectives" concept has been developed by Dr. Roger Anderson and Dr. Donald Schmalzried at the University of Wisconsin—Eau Claire. We wish to thank them for the material presented in this section.

of the student teacher in the evaluation of his own teaching. It is intended to make supervision less arbitrary and capricious than in the past. Specifically, the supervisor helps the student teacher accomplish prespecified goals through a process consisting of five components: preobservation, observation, analysis and strategy, post-conference, and analysis of conference. The supervision by objectives approach is designed to develop professionally competent teachers who:

A. regard themselves positively as teachers
B. analyze their own teaching behavior
C. establish an open mind toward supervision
D. seek supervision from peers and supervisors
E. continue to engage in self-supervision and improvement during their teaching careers.

The components of the Supervision by Objectives model are as follows:

Pre-observation Conference.

The student teacher and supervisor meet to determine the learner outcomes (objectives) to be achieved during a specific class period and subsequently how these outcomes will be preassessed and measured. Agreement is reached about what will constitute acceptable performance before the lesson is implemented. Three additional agreements are also made between the student teacher and supervisor. These are (a) the objectives for the student teacher's behavior which are to be the focus of the observation period, (b) the technique to be used to collect data about the student teacher's behavior, (such as interaction analysis or some other system for analyzing the teaching act), and (c) the role of the supervisor during the observation period (an example might be to video tape the student teacher's presentation). The emphasis is on focusing supervision practices that result in gathering decisive evidence of learner and teacher behavior rather than in making inferences or subjective observations. The pre-observation conference should occur far enough in advance of the supervision observation to allow the student teacher to reassess and modify his instructional plans.

Observation.

During the observation period data on the student teacher's behavior is collected by the supervisor through written accounts or through mechanical means, such as video taping or audio taping. The data collection is concentrated upon only those aspects of the teacher's behavior previously agreed upon by the teacher and supervisor. While the supervisor focuses on student teacher behaviors during the observation period, the student teacher concentrates on the instructional plan and the assessment of learner outcomes which were agreed upon during the pre-observation conferences.

Analysis and Strategy.

The supervisor analyzes the data collected on the student teacher's behaviors to determine if the objectives have been achieved. An example of an analysis procedure would be for the supervisor to determine the proportion of cognitive-memory questions asked by the teacher during the observation period should this have been the area singled out for attention during the pre-observation conference.

The Interaction Analysis Matrix or some other observation instruments could be utilized and analyzed. The supervisor determines the most effective strategy for conveying his analysis to the student teacher based upon the personal characteristics of the individual student teacher. During the initial pre-observation conference the supervisor must assess the student teacher's response to direct and indirect supervisory strategies. The student teacher's problems and concerns must be dealt with first. The post-observation conference must be held even if the other steps are postponed.

Post-Observation Conference.

One of the major goals during the post-observation conference is to get the student teacher to take an active part in the analysis of his own teaching and to set goals for future improvement. The student teacher and supervisor discuss the degree to which learner objectives were achieved. The supervisor may suggest alternative strategies related to the achievement of the objectives. On the other hand, the supervisor's conference plan may have to be altered or postponed if the student teacher has more immediate problems which must be dealt with during the post-observation conference.

Analysis of Conference.

In order for both the supervisor and student teacher to grow, an analysis of the conference should be undertaken. The supervisor should demonstrate the skill of self-analysis through queries about how supervision is working. Is the supervision cycle leading to improved instruction and learning? The informality of conference analysis gives the student teacher an opportunity to evaluate supervisor procedures. The student teacher's reaction provides direction about which supervisory procedures are most effective.

The key to success in the Supervision by Objectives concept is in helping the student teacher toward the following goals:

A. develop a technique for analyzing his own teaching behavior using objectives, data collection, and analysis which he can continue by himself or with peers.
B. establish his own objectives for the supervision sequence, therefore, the focus is on self-improvement rather than externally imposed changes.
C. focus on a few specific important desired changes rather than on a wide variety of minor weaknesses.
D. understand the relationship between learner outcomes and teacher behavior—between his objectives for the students and goals for himself.

The concept of a cycle of Supervision places emphasis upon the consequences of instruction in terms of pupil gain. Written accounts and observation systems are used to gather objective data. Inferences are drawn after data is collected and analyzed. In this supervision cycle, learning principles are seen as sources for generating modification of teaching methods and new instructional objectives. Supervision by Objectives appears to have within it the promise of helping to make a lasting difference in a student teacher's behavior.

SUMMARY

The glances into the future presented in this chapter are by no means all inclusive. Hopefully, however, this chapter has pointed out that the role of the student teaching supervisor is destined to become more important in future teacher education programs than has been the case in the past. This means that student teaching supervisors must work even harder at developing and refining their supervision skills. Just as there is no best way to teach, it is equally true that there is no one best way to supervise a student teacher. While there are guiding principles, each student teaching supervisor must discover his own best supervision style. The effective student teaching supervisor is one who is able to combine his personality, educational philosophy, value system, energy level, past experiences, and a host of specific supervision skills into a supervision technique that works best for him. The best way to supervise a student teacher will vary from student teacher to student teacher.

Student teachers are all individuals and a supervision strategy that works well with one may be ineffective with another. This means that the supervisor must be able to supervise in a number of different ways, and must be perceptive enough to select the best supervision strategy for each student teacher.

In order for a supervisor to develop this type of competency, he must be willing to experiment creatively with different supervisory techniques. Just as a student teacher must be willing to experiment with various teaching techniques, so must the supervisor be willing to experiment with different supervisory techniques.

Just as a teacher must continually change and refine his teaching skills and strategies, so must the supervisor constantly change and refine his supervision skills and strategies. A supervisor never reaches perfection, but rather, must constantly search for new and better ways to supervise student teachers.

Many important topics related to the supervision of clinical experiences in teacher education have been discussed in this book. Two of these concepts stand out in importance above the others. The first of these concepts is that there is no one best way to supervise student teachers who are engaged in clinical experiences. The second is that the effective supervisor must be a "student of supervision" in the same way that the effective teacher must be a "student of teaching." This means that a supervisor must constantly study and experiment with supervision. Much of this book has been aimed at trying to help the supervisor in this continuous process.

Bibliography

Supervision Books for Either the Supervising or Student Teacher

Adams, Harold P. and Frank G. Dickey. *Basic Principles of Student Teaching,* New York: American Book Company, 1956.

Andrews, L. O. *Student Teaching,* New York: Center for Applied Research in Education, 1964.

Association of Classroom Teachers. *Classroom Teachers Speak on the Classroom Teacher in the Student Teaching Program,* NEA, 1970.

Bennie, William A. *Cooperation for Better Student Teaching,* Minneapolis: Burgess, 1966.

Bennie, William A. *Supervising Clinical Experiences in the Classroom,* New York: Harper and Row, 1972.

Boney, Joan and Lois Rhea. *Guide to Student Teaching in Music,* New Jersey: Prentice-Hall, Inc., 1970.

Brown, Thomas J. *Student Teaching in a Secondary School/Guiding a Student Teacher,* New York: Harper & Row, 1968.

Brown, Thomas J. and Serafina F. Banich. *Student Teaching in an Elementary School/Guiding a Student Teacher,* New York: Harper & Brothers, 1962.

Burr, James B., Lowry W. Harding and Leland B. Jacobs. *Student Teaching in the Elementary School,* New York: Appleton-Century-Crofts. Second edition 1958.

Byers, Loretta and Elizabeth Irish. *Success in Student Teaching,* Boston: D.C. Heath and Company, 1961.

Cogan, Morris L. *Clinical Supervision,* Boston: Houghton-Mifflin, 1973.

Cook, Kermit and Others. *Student Teaching in the Secondary School,* Dubuque, Iowa: W. C. Brown Company, 1954.

Crow, Lester D. and Alice Crow: *The Student Teacher in the Elementary School,* New York: David McKay Company, 1965.

Crow, Lester D. and Alice Crow. *The Student Teacher in the Secondary School,* New York: David McKay Company, 1964.

Curtis, Dwight K. and Leonard O. Andrews. *Guiding Your Student Teacher,* Englewood Cliffs: Prentice-Hall, 1954.

Devor, John W. *The Experience of Student Teaching,* New York: the Macmillan Company, 1964.

Drayer, Adam M. *Problems and Methods in High School Teaching,* Boston: D.C. Health & Company, 1963.

Dussault, Gilles. *Theory of Supervision in Teacher Education,* New York: Teachers College Press, Columbia University, 1970.

Flowers, J. F. (ed.) *School and Community Laboratory Experiences in Teacher Education,* Washington: American Association of Colleges for Teacher Education, 1948.

Goldhammer, Robert. *Clinical Supervision,* Holt, Rinehart, Winston, 1969.

Green, Gwynn A. *Problem Situations in Student Teaching,* New York: Bureau of Publications, Teachers College, Columbia University, 1959.

Grim, Paul R. and John U. Michaelis. *The Student Teacher in the Secondary School,* New York: Prentice-Hall, Inc., 1953.

Gruhn, William T. *Student Teaching in the Secondary School,* New York: Ronald Press, 1954.

173

Haines, Aleyne C. *Guiding the Student Teaching Process in Elementary Education,* Chicago: Rand McNally, 1960.

Henry, Marvin A. and W. Wayne Beasley. *Supervising Student Teachers the Professional Way,* Indiana: Sycamore Press, 1972.

Hoffman, E. *Anxious Days,* Illinois: The Interstate Printers and Publishers, Inc., 1971.

Houston, W. R. and F. H. Blackington, III, and H. C. Southworth. *Professional Growth Through Student Teaching,* Columbus: Charles E. Merrill, 1965.

Hunter, Elizabeth. *The Cooperating Teacher at Work: Case Studies of Critical Incidents,* New York: Teachers College, Columbia University, 1962.

Hunter, Elizabeth and E. Amidon. *Cases and Comments, Student Teaching,* New York: Holt, Rinehart and Winston, 1964.

Johnson, James A. *A Brief History of Student Teaching,* DeKalb, Illinois: Creative Education Materials, 1968.

Johnson, James A. and L. D. Deprin. *Elementary Student Teaching,* Glenview: Scott Foresmen, 1971.

Johnson, James A. and R. C. Anderson. *Secondary Student Teaching,* Glenview: Scott Foresman, 1971.

Johnson, Jim, and Floyd Perry. *Readings in Student Teaching—for those who work with student teachers,* Dubuque: Wm. C. Brown, 1973.

Keach, Everett T. Jr. *Elementary School Student Teaching: A Casebook,* New York: John Wiley & Sons, 1966.

Lamb, Pose. *The Student Teaching Process in Elementary Schools,* Columbus: Charles E. Merrill, 1964.

Lindsey, Margaret and William T. Gruhn. *Student Teaching in the Elementary School,* New York: Ronald Press, 1957.

McDonald, Blanche and Leslie Nelson. *Successful Classroom Control,* Dubuque, Iowa: W. C. Brown Company, 1955.

McGeoch, Dorothy M. *Direct Experiences in Teacher Education: A Story of Three Programs,* New York: Bureau of Publications, Teachers College, Columbia University, 1953.

McGuire, Vincent, Robert B. Myers and Charles L. Currance. *Your Student Teaching in the Secondary School,* Boston: Allyn and Bacon, Inc., 1959.

Merrill, Edward C. *Professional Student Teaching Programs: A Handbook for the Student Teachers, Cooperating School Personnel, and College and University Sponsors,* Danville, Illinois: Interstate Printers and Publishers, 1973.

Michaelis, John U. and Paul R. Grim. *The Student Teacher in the Elementary School,* New York: Prentice-Hall, Inc., 1953.

Milner, Ernest J. *You and Your Student Teacher,* New York: Teachers College, Columbia University, 1954.

Morine, Greta and Robert Spaulding. *Discovering New Dimensions in the Student Teaching Process,* Pennsylvania: Intext Educational Publishers, 1971.

Myers, George R. and W. J. Walsh. *Student Teaching and Internship in Today's Secondary Schools,* Columbus: Charles E. Merrill Books, Inc., 1964.

Neal, Charles D. *Student Teacher at Work,* Minnesota: Burgess Publishing Company, 1971.

Nelson, Leslie and Blanche McDonald. *Guide to Student Teaching,* Dubuque, Iowa: Wm. C. Brown Company, 1958.

Perrodin, Alex F. *The Student Teacher's Reader,* Chicago: Rand McNally, 1966.

Provus, Malcolm. *Teaching for Relevance,* Northbrook, Illinois: Whitehall Company, 1970.

Rosenstein, Irwin and G. J. Hase. *Student Teaching in Physical Education,* New Jersey: Prentice-Hall, Inc., 1971.

Schorling, Raleigh and Howard T. Batchelder. *Student Teaching in Secondary Schools,* New York: McGraw-Hill, Fourth edition, 1964.

Schultz, Raymond E. *Student Teaching in the Secondary Schools,* New York: Harcourt, Brace and Company, 1959.

Steeves, Frank. Issues in Student Teaching: *A Casebook with Related Problems in Teacher Education,* New York: The Odyssey Press, 1963.

Stratemeyer, Florence B. and Margaret Lindsey. *Working with Student Teachers,* New York: Bureau of Publications, Teachers College, Columbia University, 1958.

Swalls, Fred. *Legal Aspects of Student Teaching,* Dansville, Illinois: Interstate, second edition, 1971.

T.E.P.S.A. *New Order in Student Teaching,* Washington: National Commission on Teacher Education and Professional Standards, 1967.

T.E.P.S. *Who's in Charge Here?,* (A Discussion Paper Fixing Responsibilities for Student Teaching) Washington: National Commission on Teacher Education and Professional Standards, 1966.

Van Dalen, Deobold B. and Robert W. Brittell. *Looking Ahead to Teaching,* Boston: Allyn and Bacon, Inc., 1959.

Wiggins, Sam P. *The Student Teacher in Action,* Boston: Allyn and Bacon, Inc., 1957.

Wingo, G. Max and Raleigh Schorling. *Elementary School Student Teaching,* New York: McGraw-Hill, Third edition, 1961.

Woods, Thomas, J. Mauries and Bruce U. Dick. *Student Teaching: The Entrance to Professional Physical Education,* New York: Academic Press, 1973.

EDUCATIONAL JOURNALS WITH FREQUENT OR OCCASIONAL ARTICLES ON SUPERVISION

Administrator's Notebook: Monthly, $3.00, University of Chicago, Midwest Administrative Center, 5835 Kimbark Avenue, Chicago, Illinois 60637.

American Education: Monthly, $4.50, U.S. Government Printing Office, Superintendent of Documents, Washington D.C. 20036.

American Education Research Journal: Quarterly, $6.00, American Education Research Association, 1126 16th Street N.W., Washington, D.C. 20036.

Arithmetic Teacher—8 copies/year, $10.00, National Council of Teachers of Mathematics, 1201 16th Street N.W., Washington, D.C. 20036.

Audio-Visual Instruction: Monthly $12.00, N E A, Department of Audio-Visual Instruction, 1201 16th Street N.W., Washington, D.C. 20036.

British Journal of Educational Psychology: Quarterly, $9.55, A B P Andover, North Way, Andover, Hampshire, England.

Business Education Forum: National Business Education Association, c/o N E A, 1201 16th Street N.W., Washington, D.C. 20036.

Business Education World: 5/year, McGraw-Hill, Inc., Gregg Division, 1221 Avenue of the Americas, New York, New York 10020.

California Journal of Educational Research: 5/year, $10.00, California Teachers Association, 1705 Murchison Drive, Burlingame, California 94010.

California Journal of Teacher Education: St. Mary's College, P.O. Box 406, Moraga, California 94575.

Changing Education: Quarterly, $5.00, 1012 14th Street N.W., Washington, D.C. 20005.

Clearing House: Monthly, $5.00, Fairleigh Dickinson University, Teaneck, New Jersey 07666.

Contemporary Education: 6/year, free, Indiana State University, 118 North Sixth Street, Terre Haute, Indiana 47809.

Education Forum: Quarterly, $5.00, Kappa Delta Pi, Box A, West Lafayette, Indiana 47906.

Education and Psychology Measurement: Box 6907, College Station, Durham, North Carolina 27708.

Educational Leadership: Monthly, $5.50, Association for Supervision and Curriculum Development, 1201 16th Street N.W., Washington, D.C. 20036.

Elementary School Journal: Monthly, $8.00, University of Chicago Press, 5801 Ellis Avenue, Chicago, Illinois 60637.

English Journal: Monthly, $12.00, National Council of Teachers of English, 1111 Kenyon Road, Urbana, Illinois 61801.

Harvard Educational Review: Bi-monthly, $8.00, Harvard University, Graduate School of Education, Longfellow Hall, 13 Appian Way, Cambridge, Massachusetts 02138.

High School Journal: Monthly, $5.00, University of North Carolina Press, Box 510, Chapel Hill, North Carolina 27515.

Improving College and University Teaching: Oregon State University, 101 Wade Hall, Corvallis, Oregon 97331.

Instructor: 10/year, $7.00, F. A. Owen Publishing Company, 5 Bank Street, Dansville, New York 14437.

Integrated Education: Bi-Monthly, $5.00, Integrated Education Association, 3435 Dearborn Street, Chicago, Illinois 60604.

Journal of Education: Quarterly, $5.00, Boston University, School of Education, 765 Common Wealth Avenue, Boston, Massachusetts 02215.

Journal of Educational Data Processing: Bi-Monthly, $11.00, Educational Systems Corporation, 721 Capitol Mall, Sacramento, California 95814.

Journal of Educational Psychology: Bi-Monthly, $10.00, American Psychology Association, 1200 17th Street N.W., Washington, D.C. 20036.

Journal of Educational Research: Monthly, $10.00, P.O. Box 1605, Madison, Wisconsin 53701.

Journal of Experimental Education: Quarterly, $10.00, Dembar Education Research Services, Inc., P.O. Box 1605, Madison, Wisconsin 53701.

Journal of Health, Physical Education, and Recreation: Monthly, $15.00, International Council of H P E R, 1201 16th Street N.W., Washington, D.C. 20036.

Journal of Home Economics: Monthly, $12.00, American Home Economics Association, 1600 20th Street, N.W., Washington, D.C. 20009.

Journal of Negro Education: Quarterly, $5.00, Howard University, Bureau of Education Research, Washington, D.C. 20001.

Journal of Research and Development in Education: Quarterly, $7.00, College of Education, University of Georgia, Baldwin Hall, Room 122, Athens, Georgia, 30601.

Journal of Research in Music Education: Quarterly, $6.00, Society for Research in Music Education, Music Educator's National Conference, 1201 16th Street N.W., Washington, D.C. 20036.

Journal of Research in Science Teaching: Quarterly, $10.00, John Wiley and

Sons, One Wiley Drive, Somerset, New Jersey 08873.

Journal of School Health: American School Health Association, 515 East Main Street, Kent, Ohio 44240.

Journal of Secondary Education: Monthly, $5.00, Journal Subscription Department, California Association of Secondary School Administration, Suite A, 1550 Rollins Road, Burlingame, California 94010.

Journal of Teacher Education: Quarterly, $10.00, American Association of Colleges for Teacher Education, AACTE, One Dupont Circle, Washington, D.C. 20036.

Mathematics Teacher: 8/year, $10.00, National Council of Teachers of Mathematics, 1201 16th Street N.W., Washington, D.C. 20036.

Music Educator's Journal: 9/year, $4.00, Music Educator's National Conference, 1201 16th Street N.W., Washington, D.C. 20036.

N A S S P Bulletin: 9/year, $4.00 (members), National Association of Secondary School Principals, 1904 Association Drive, Reston, Virginia 20091.

Nation's Schools: Monthly, $15.00, McGraw-Hill, Inc., 230 West Monroe Street, Chicago, Illinois 60606.

National Elementary Principal: Bi-Monthly, $20.00, National Association of Elementary Principals, 1801 North Moore Street, Arlington, Virginia 22209.

North Central Association Quarterly: Quarterly, $6.00, North Central Association of Colleges and Secondary Schools, 5454 South Shore Drive, Chicago, Illinois 60615.

Peabody Journal of Education: Quarterly, $8.00, Peabody College for Teachers, Nashville, Tennessee 37203.

Phi Delta Kappan: Monthly, $8.00, Phi Delta Kappa, Inc., 8th and Union Avenue, Box 789, Bloomington, Indiana 47401.

Reading Teacher: Monthly, $15.00, International Reading Association, 6 Tyre Avenue, Newark, Delaware, 19711.

Research in the Teaching of English: Semi-Annual, $3.00, National Council of Teachers of English, 1111 Kenyon Road, Urbana, Illinois 61801.

School and Community: Available only to members, Monthly, Missouri State Teachers Association, P.O. Box 458, Columbia, Missouri 65201.

School Arts Magazine: Monthly, $7.00, Davis Publications, Inc., Printers Building, Worcester, Massachusetts 01608.

School Review: University of Chicago Press, 5750 Ellis Avenue, Chicago, Illinois 60637.

School Science and Mathematics: Monthly, $8.00, Central Association of Science and Mathematics Teachers, Box 246, Bloomington, Indiana 47401.

Science Education—University of Tampa, Tampa, Florida 33606.

Studies in Art Education: 3/year, $4.50, National Art Educator's Association, 1201 16th Street N.W., Washington, D.C. 20036.

Teacher Educator: 3/year, free, Teacher's College, Ball State University, Muncie, Indiana 47306.

Teacher's College Record: Quarterly, $10.00, Teacher's College, Columbia University, 525 West 120th Street, New York, New York, 10027.

Today's Education: Monthly, $7.20, N E A, 1201 16th Street, N.W., Washington D.C. 20036.

Association of Teacher Educators Publications

The previous section of this bibliography illustrated that a number of professional associations publish journals that frequently contain articles of interest and value to the supervisor. Several, in addition, have published materials that may have particular reference to the tasks of the various personnel engaged in field experiences. The publications of the Association of Teacher Educators (formerly the Association for Student Teaching) have such consistent pertinence and are of such particular value to all of the various parties involved in the student teaching process that they are listed in the following section:

BULLETINS

#37 Teacher Leadership: A Model for Change—Andrew (1974) $4.00
#36 Winds of Change: Teacher Education for the Open Area School—Ross, Beaven, Ishler and Ishler, Spodek, Manolakes, Binko, and Gilstrap (1974) $3.00
#35 To Cope With the Current—Martin (1974) $3.00
#34 Students' Rights: A Guide to the Rights of Children, Youth, and Future Teachers—Haberman (1973) $2.50
#33 Guiding Student Teaching Experiences in a Cooperative Structure—Kerber and Protheroe (1973) $2.50
#32 Teacher Preparation: Supervision and Performance—Spanjer (1972) $2.50
#31 Teachers Should Be Human Too—Andrew (1972) $2.50
#30 The Teaching Clinic: A Team Approach to the Improvement of Teaching— Olsen, Barbour, and Michalak (1971) $1.25
#29 Teaching is Communicating: Nonverbal Language in the Classroom— Galloway (1970) $1.00
#28 Supervisory Conference as Individualized Teaching—Bebb, Low, and Waterman (1969) $1.25
#27 The Student Teacher and Professional Activities—Loftis (1967) $1.25
#25 The Student Teacher and Team Teaching—Fullerton and Griffith (1966) $1.25
#21 The Student Teacher's Experiences in the Community—Blair and Erickson (1964) $1.00
 #1 Guiding Student Teaching Experiences—Hilliard and Durrance (1968) $1.00

RESEARCH BULLETINS

#12 Alternative Approaches to Student Involvement in Teacher Education: Three Research Studies—Greenstein and Greenstein, Ahnell and Templeton, Ishler (1973) $2.25
#11 Guidelines for Selection of Students into Programs of Teacher Education— Haberman (1972) $1.50

#10 Interaction Analysis: Selected Papers—Furst, Sandefur and Bressler, Johnston (1971) $1.50

#9 Microteaching: Selected Papers—Cooper and Allen, Schurk (1971) $1.50

#8 Simulation as an Instructional Alternative in Teacher Preparation—Cruickshank (1971) $1.25

#7 The Director of Student Teaching: Characteristics and Responsibilities—Miller, Griffith, and Martin (1969) $1.50

COMMISSION PUBLICATIONS

New Directions in Certification—Andrews (1971) $1.50

Performance-Based Certification of School Personnel—Burdin and Reagan, editors (1971) $1.75

Teacher Education: Future Directions—Report of 1970 Conference Presentations, Lindsey, editor (1970) $4.00

POSITION PAPERS

Guidelines to Clinical Experiences in Teacher Education—A Position Paper (revised 1973) $2.25

The Supervising Teacher: Standards for Selection and Function, Position Paper 1, $ .75

The College Supervisor: Standards for Selection and Function, Position Paper 2, $ .75

YEARBOOKS (DISCONTINUED WITH 47TH YEARBOOK)

Internships in Teacher Education, 47th Yearbook, $4.75

Mental Health and Teacher Education, 46th Yearbook, $4.75

Professional Growth In-Service of the Supervising Teacher, 45th Yearbook, $4.75

Theoretical Bases for Professional Laboratory Experiences in Teacher Education, 44th Yearbook, $3.50

HOW TO ORDER: Prices quoted are for single copies. Discounts on quantities of same title: 10–49 copies, 10%; 50 or more, 15%. Order must be prepaid unless on official institutional purchase order form. Shipping and handling will be added to all billed orders. Make check or money order payable to ATE. Current prices quoted, subject to change without notice.

Publication orders and membership inquiries should be addressed to: Association of Teacher Educators, Suite 1201, 1701 K Street, N.W., Washington, D.C. 20006